Bond

No.1 for exam success

AF077802

Verbal Reasoning

Assessment Papers

8–9 years

OXFORD
UNIVERSITY PRESS

OXFORD
UNIVERSITY PRESS

Great Clarendon Street, Oxford, OX2 6DP, United Kingdom

Oxford University Press is a department of the University of Oxford. It furthers the University's objective of excellence in research, scholarship, and education by publishing worldwide. Oxford is a registered trade mark of Oxford University Press in the UK and in certain other countries

Text © J M Bond and Frances Down 2015

The moral rights of the authors have been asserted

First published in 2015
This edition published in 2021

All rights reserved. No part of this publication may be reproduced, stored in a retrieval system, or transmitted, in any form or by any means, without the prior permission in writing of Oxford University Press, or as expressly permitted by law, by licence or under terms agreed with the appropriate reprographics rights organization. Enquiries concerning reproduction outside the scope of the above should be sent to the Rights Department, Oxford University Press, at the address above.

You must not circulate this work in any other form and you must impose this same condition on any acquirer

British Library Cataloguing in Publication Data
Data available

978-0-19-277991-5

10 9 8 7 6

Paper used in the production of this book is a natural, recyclable product made from wood grown in sustainable forests.
The manufacturing process conforms to the environmental regulations of the country of origin.

Printed in China

Acknowledgements

The publishers would like to thank the following for permissions to use copyright material:

Page make-up: OKS Prepress, India
Cover illustrations: Lo Cole

Although we have made every effort to trace and contact all copyright holders before publication this has not been possible in all cases. If notified, the publisher will rectify any errors or omissions at the earliest opportunity.

Links to third party websites are provided by Oxford in good faith and for information only. Oxford disclaims any responsibility for the materials contained in any third party website referenced in this work.

The manufacturer's authorised representative in the EU for product safety is Oxford University Press España S.A. of El Parque Empresarial San Fernando de Henares, Avenida de Castilla, 2 – 28830 Madrid (www.oup.es/en or product.safety@oup.com). OUP España S.A. also acts as importer into Spain of products made by the manufacturer.

Before you get started

What is Bond?

This book is part of the Bond Assessment Papers series for verbal reasoning, which provides a **thorough and continuous course in verbal reasoning** from ages six to twelve. It builds up verbal reasoning skills from book to book over the course of the series.

What does this book cover?

Verbal reasoning questions can be grouped into four distinct groups: sorting words, selecting words, anagrams, coded sequences and logic. This book practises a wide range of questions appropriate to the age group drawn from all these categories. One of the key features of Bond Assessment Papers is that each one practises **a very wide variety of skills and question types** so that children are always challenged to think – and don't get bored repeating the same question type again and again. We believe that variety is the key to effective learning. It helps children 'think on their feet' and cope with the unexpected.

The age given on the cover is for guidance only. As the papers are designed to be reasonably challenging for the age group, any one child may naturally find him or herself working above or below the stated age. The important thing is that children are always encouraged by their performance. Working at the right level is the key to this.

What does the book contain?

- **20 papers –** each one contains 45 questions.
- **Scoring devices –** there are score boxes next to the questions and a Progress Chart at the back. The chart is a visual and motivating way for children to see how they are doing. Encouraging them to colour in the chart as they go along and to try to beat their last score can be highly effective!
- **Next Steps Planner –** advice on what to do after finishing the papers can be found on the inside back cover.
- **Answers –** located in an easily-removed central pull-out section.

How can you use this book?

One of the great strengths of Bond Assessment Papers is their flexibility. They can be used at home, school and by tutors to:

- provide regular verbal reasoning practice in **bite-sized chunks**
- **highlight strengths and weaknesses** in the core skills
- identify **individual needs**
- set **homework**
- set **timed formal practice tests –** allow about 30 minutes.

It is best to start at the beginning and work through the papers in order.

What does a score mean and how can it be improved?

If children colour in the Progress Chart at the back, this will give an idea of how they are doing. The Next Steps Planner inside the back cover will help you to decide what to do next to help a child progress. We suggest that it is always valuable to go over any wrong answers with children.

Don't forget the website...!

Visit www.assessmentpapers.co.uk for lots of advice, information and suggestions on everything to do with Bond, helping children to do their best, and exams.

Paper 1

Underline the pair of words most similar in meaning.

Example come, go roam, wander fear, fare

1 alley, lane real, false back, forward

2 good, bad bake, oven heavy, weighty

3 beat, lose bite, nip bath, room

4 nose, face shallow, river correct, right

5 come, go sorry, glad closed, shut

5

Find the three-letter word which can be added to the letters in capitals to make a new word. The new word will complete the sentence sensibly.

Example The cat sprang onto the MO. USE

6 SN days make a week. _____

7 We put SS on our feet. _____

8 He FED his cup to the brim. _____

9 They SED me the way to the town. _____

10 I would like to hear a story BEE I go to sleep. _____

5

Underline two words, one from each group, that go together to form a new word. The word in the first group always comes first.

Example (hand, green, for) (light, house, sure)

11 (is, be, it) (bed, low, high)

12 (shut, open, in) (side, back, air)

13 (for, form, fear) (car, got, back)

14 (toe, finger, hand) (rip, tip, side)

15 (face, hair, hand) (shave, some, were)

5

Change the first word of the third pair in the same way as the other pairs to give a new word.

Example	bind, hind	bare, hare	but, hut
16	art, part	ale, pale	ant, _____
17	ill, till	all, tall	ear, _____
18	pick, prick	feed, freed	tied, _____
19	ran, rain	man, main	pan _____
20	top, stop	tar, star	tab, _____

5

Fill in the missing letters. The alphabet has been written out to help you.

A B C D E F G H I J K L M N O P Q R S T U V W X Y Z

Example AB is to CD as PQ is to RS.

21 A is to D as G is to ____.

22 3B is to 4D as 5F is to ____.

23 ABD is to BCE as CDF is to ____.

24 MAB is to NBC as OCD is to ____.

25 9AB is to 8CD as 7EF is to ____.

5

Fill in the crosswords so that all the given words are included. You have been given one letter as a clue in each crossword.

26

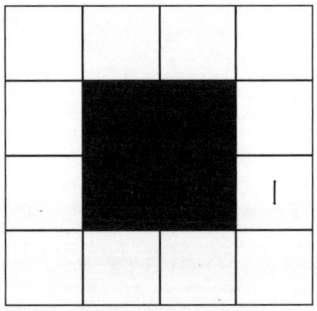

edit, hint, home, tent

27

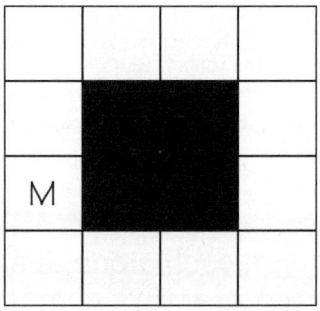

ends, moss, term, time

28

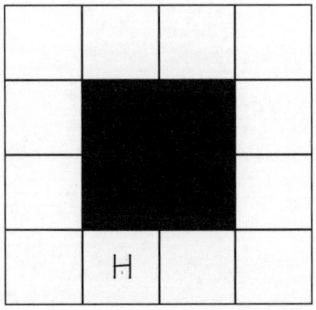

heap, ship, wags, wish

3

Fill in the missing number in each sequence.

	Example	2	4	6	8	10
29	12	15		_____	21	24
30	1996	1998		_____	2002	2004
31	20	17		14	11	_____
32	4.5	5.0		5.5	6.0	_____
33	19	_____		22	25	29
34	20	18		15	11	_____

6

If the code for PEARS is 13579, what are the codes for the following words?

35 ARE _____ **36** RAP _____

37 SPA _____ **38** SEE _____

39 PEA _____

What do these codes stand for?

40 91357 _____ **41** 511357 _____

7

Here are some TV programmes.

14:00 Play School
14:15 Cartoons
15:30 Think Twice
16:00 The School on the Hill
16:30 News

How many minutes do these programmes last?

42 Play School ___ minutes **43** Cartoons ___ minutes

44 Think Twice ___ minutes **45** The School on the Hill ___ minutes

4

Now go to the Progress Chart to record your score! **Total** 45

Paper 2

Underline the word in brackets closest in meaning to the word in capitals.

Example UNHAPPY (unkind death laughter <u>sad</u> friendly)

1 CLEVER (school bright pupil stupid trick)

2 QUICK (slow fast speed walk step)

3 LAUGH (cry taught funny chuckle humour)

4 MODERN (easy today young new trend)

5 SIMPLE (crazy silly hard easy straight)

5

Find the missing number by using the two numbers outside the brackets in the same way as the other sets of numbers.

Example 2 [8] 4 3 [18] 6 5 [<u>25</u>] 5

6 3 [9] 6 4 [6] 2 1 [__] 6

7 5 [10] 2 4 [12] 3 6 [__] 2

8 2 [5] 3 7 [8] 1 2 [__] 8

9 7 [6] 1 5 [3] 2 8 [__] 4

10 15 [5] 3 21 [3] 7 16 [__] 4

5

Find the letter which will end the first word and start the second word.

Example peac (<u>h</u>) ome

11 han (__) oor

12 mat (__) ver

13 sal (__) ill

14 duc (__) ite

15 mas (__) est

5

Fill in the crosswords so that all the given words are included. You have been given one letter as a clue in each crossword.

16

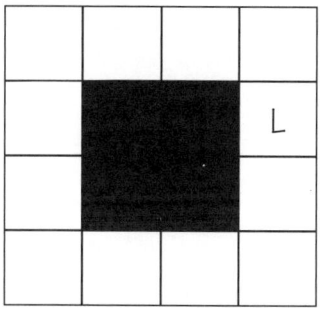

cats, camp, plum, sham

17

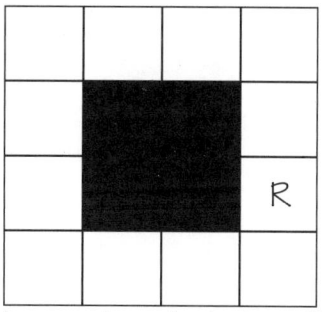

beam, bend, dark, milk

18

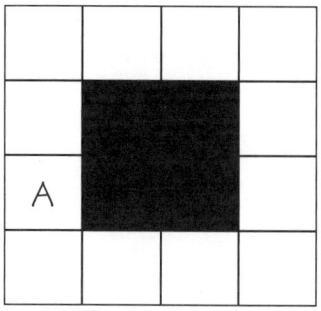

bank, bear, king, ring

3

Underline two words, one from each group, that go together to form a new word. The word in the first group always comes first.

Example (hand, green, for) (light, house, sure)

19 (bed, for, right) (tub, cot, side)

20 (near, after, under) (some, ground, set)

21 (in, an, it) (left, form, just)

22 (far, near, out) (law, police, here)

23 (far, for, ran) (take, give, us)

5

Change the first word into the last word by changing one letter at a time and making a new word in the middle.

Example CASE CASH LASH

24 PANE _____ PINK

25 COMB _____ HOME

26 HOPE _____ COPY

27 HATE _____ MITE

28 COLD _____ GILD

5

If the code for POSTER is 235689, what are the codes for the following words?

29 STOP _____ **30** SET _____

What do these codes stand for?

31 632 _____ **32** 6355 _____

33 899 _____

5

Choose the word or phrase that makes each sentence true.

Example A LIBRARY always has (posters, a carpet, books, DVDs, stairs).

34 A HOUSE always has (a garage, curtains, walls, a doorbell, a fence).

35 A LAKE always has (ducks, boats, fish, swans, water).

36 A CITY always has (farms, buildings, an airport, an underground, a river).

37 A KITCHEN always has (a table, chairs, a stove, plants, a radio).

38 A SCHOOL always has (a cafeteria, a nurse, students, a swimming pool, a bus).

5

Underline the two words which are made from the same letters.

Example TAP PET TEA POT EAT

39 MEAT TIME TUNE TEAM MUST

40 NUT TEN NET TAN NOT

41 TEST STAB LAST LOST SALT

3

Remove one letter from the word in capitals to leave a new word.
The meaning of the new word is given in the clue.

Example	AUNT	an insect	ant
42	FARM	not near	_____
43	HARM	a piece of meat	_____
44	GROUND	shaped like a ball	_____
45	THAN	you get it from sunbathing	_____

4

Now go to the Progress Chart to record your score! **Total** 45

Paper 3

Underline the two words which are the odd ones out in the following groups of words.

Example	black	king	purple	green	house
1	quiet	peaceful	crowd	calm	concert
2	small	short	enlarge	brief	expand
3	sea	harbour	ocean	pier	lake
4	sturdy	weak	strong	healthy	ill
5	walk	swim	stride	dive	march

5

Find the three-letter word which can be added to the letters in capitals to make a new word. The new word will complete the sentence sensibly.

Example The cat sprang onto the MO. USE

6 The weather was W and sunny. _____

7 He SCHED high and low for the remote control. _____

8 I've got some nice, new PYAS to wear. _____

9 My favourite fruit is an APRI. _____

10 The octopus caught him with its TACLES. _____

5

Which one letter can be added to the front of all of these words to make new words?

	Example	c<u>a</u>re	c<u>a</u>t	c<u>r</u>ate	c<u>a</u>ll
11	__late	__lease	__ony	__each
12	__right	__ig	__all	__ean
13	__how	__et	__poon	__nake
14	__elt	__eal	__at	__oan
15	__hall	__eal	__mall	__nail

5

Add one letter to the word in capital letters to make a new word. The meaning of the new word is given in the clue.

Example	PLAN	simple	<u>plain</u>
16	TROT	a fish	_____
17	NOSE	the opposite of silence	_____
18	TICK	the opposite of thin	_____
19	LATE	used to put our food on	_____
20	SORT	different types of games	_____

5

Fill in the crosswords so that all the given words are included. You have been given one letter as a clue in each crossword.

21

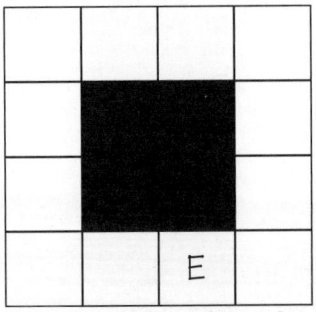

keep, mark, mist, trip

22

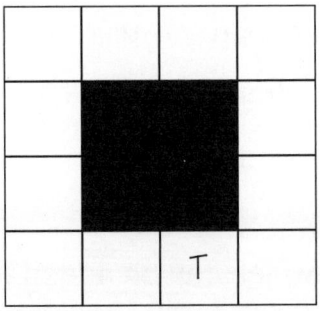

date, fire, half, hard

23

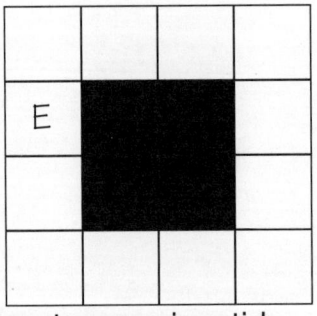

part, pear, ripe, tide

3

Fill in the missing number in each sequence.

	Example	2	4	6	8	10
24	3	6	9	__	15
25	12	10	8	__	4
26	12	24	__	48	60
27	21	32	43	__	65
28	121	232	__	454	565

5

These words have been written in code, but the codes are not under the right words.

TOO	OUT	TOT	TO	UP
72	722	247	46	727

Write the correct code for each word.

29 TOO _____ **30** OUT _____

31 TOT _____ **32** TO _____

33 UP _____

5

If a = 1, b = 2, c = 3, find the sum of:

34 a + b + c = _____ **35** c + 2b = _____

36 2a + 2b = _____

3

Underline the one word which **cannot be made** from the letters of the word in capital letters.

	Example	STATIONERY	stones	tyres	ration	nation	noisy
37	CONSIDER	cried	nice	dear	rice	coin
38	LOWEST	low	west	flow	sew	owl
39	TEACHER	eaten	chat	ear	are	crate
40	INSIDE	den	snide	end	dine	need

4

In each line, underline the word that has its letters in alphabetical order.

41	gas	guzzle	grunt	got
42	apple	ant	ask	ale
43	clever	caution	care	cry
44	deal	dint	dream	drink
45	flow	flea	frank	frog

5

Now go to the Progress Chart to record your score! **Total** 45

Paper 4

Find and underline the two words which need to change places for each sentence to make sense.

Example She went to <u>letter</u> the <u>write</u>.

1 The tail wagged her dog when she saw the treat.

2 My sister told my mother to finish her homework.

3 I like to read a bed before book.

4 At my birthday cake we ate ice cream and party.

5 My mum takes the office to her bus.

5

Underline two words, one from each group, that go together to form a new word. The word in the first group always comes first.

Example (hand, <u>green</u>, for) (light, <u>house</u>, sure)

6 (wood, light, sea) (day, tree, weed)

7 (earth, glass, sand) (sun, castle, rain)

8 (well, work, pail) (shop, cut, know)

9 (foot, glove, hand) (knee, head, shake)

10 (under, over, through) (sky, place, water)

5

Fill in the crosswords so that all the given words are included. You have been given one letter as a clue in each crossword.

11

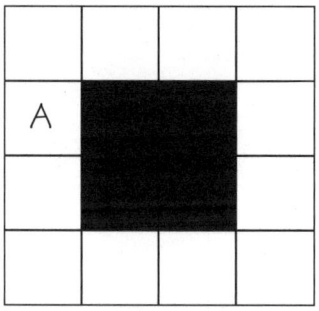

keen, park, port, torn

12

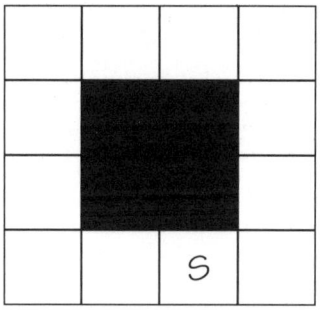

easy, heal, hole, lazy

2

Underline one word in the brackets which is most opposite in meaning to the word in capitals.

Example WIDE (broad vague long <u>narrow</u> motorway)

13 HEALTHY (good doctor hospital ill patient)

14 TEACHER (school pupil lesson term tutor)

15 FRIEND (pal mate foe ally neighbour)

16 MANY (more lots few crowd half)

17 WHOLE (entire part some complete full)

5

Find the three-letter word which can be added to the letters in capitals to make a new word. The new word will complete the sentence sensibly.

Example The cat sprang onto the MO. <u>USE</u>

18 A baby is an INT. _____

19 A baby goes out in a P. _____

20 A baby CLS on the floor. _____

21 A baby plays with a TLE. _____

22 A baby sits in a HIGHCH. _____

5

Add one letter to the word in capital letters to make a new word. The meaning of the new word is given in the clue.

Example PLAN simple plain

23 WAS an insect _____

24 HOP to expect the best _____

25 LOW the opposite of fast _____

26 HAT to stop _____

27 RAN it pours _____ 5

Complete the following expressions by underlining the missing word.

Example Frog is to tadpole as swan is to (duckling, baby, cygnet).

28 Sun is to sunk as pin is to (sink, pin, pink).

29 Eye is to see as ear is to (speak, hear, nose).

30 Bed is to bead as led is to (late, lead, deal).

31 Top is to bottom as right is to (correct, under, left).

32 Speak is to talk as consider is to (count, think, moan).

33 Ail is to bail as ill is to (sill, will, bill). 6

34 boy but why she sty

If these words were written backwards, which word would now come first in alphabetical order?

_____ 1

These words have been written in code, but the codes are not under the right words.

BE	BEG	BIN	BEGIN	BEE
244	24538	24	245	238

Write the correct code for each word.

35 BE _____ 36 BEG _____ 37 BIN _____ 38 BEE _____ 39 BEGIN _____ 5

If a = 3, b = 2, d = 6, e = 8, f = 10, find the value of:

40 2f − 2a = ___ **41** 2e − 2b = ___ 2

Sue and Omar wear yellow tops.

Lee and Omar wear green trousers.

Sue and Jess wear brown trousers.

Jess and Lee wear red tops.

Who wears:

42 a yellow top and brown trousers? _____

43 a red top and green trousers? _____

44 a yellow top and green trousers? _____

45 a red top and brown trousers? _____ 4

Now go to the Progress Chart to record your score! **Total** 45

Paper 5

Which one letter can be added to the front of all of these words to make new words.

	Example	c<u></u>are	c<u></u>at	c<u></u>rate	c<u></u>all
1	___arm	___and	___as	___ollow	
2	___old	___hill	___loud	___an	
3	___read	___ream	___ark	___ome	
4	___and	___right	___ear	___each	
5	___rim	___ower	___ride	___lant	

5

The train was due in at 10:50. It was 10 minutes late.

6 When did it arrive? _____

I left home at 18:15. It took me 20 minutes to walk to the cinema.

7 When did I get there? _____

A pudding takes 50 minutes to cook. I want it to be ready for 13:00.

8 When must I put it into the oven? _____ 3

If these words were placed in alphabetical order, which word would come first?

9	Monday	Thursday	Wednesday	Friday	Tuesday	_____
10	May	January	March	February	April	_____
11	giraffe	elephant	mouse	horse	dog	_____
12	plane	helicopter	kite	balloon	rocket	_____ 4

Underline one word in the brackets which is most opposite in meaning to the word in capitals.

Example WIDE (broad vague long <u>narrow</u> motorway)

13 WARM (hot cold icy sun fine)

14 BLACK (dark brown white sooty coal)

15 HIDE (lost last find secret conceal)

16 MORE (less many few lots plenty)

17 FIRST (top bottom side last enough) 5

Underline two words which are made from the same letters.

Example TAP PET <u>TEA</u> POT <u>EAT</u>

18	MAUL	PART	MAKE	TRAM	TRAP
19	AGES	ALES	APES	SAGE	SAND
20	LIMP	LEAP	PEEP	PEAL	PEARL
21	WARN	WARM	WARD	WARP	DRAW
22	LATE	LINT	TALE	TILE	FILE

5

Remove one letter from the word in capitals to leave a new word. The meaning of the new word is given in the clue.

Example AUNT an insect ant

23 ROAD a stick _____

24 PINT something we use when sewing _____

25 TINT a metal _____

26 CODE a type of fish _____

27 HARM part of our body _____

5

Underline the number that completes each sequence.

28 4 is to 16 as 16 is to (72, 64, 60)

29 3 is to 12 as 12 is to (24, 36, 48)

30 32 is to 16 as 16 is to (4, 8, 12)

31 55 is to 11 as 60 is to (11, 12, 14)

32 100 is to 50 as 90 is to (55, 40, 45)

5

These words have been written in code, but the codes are not under the right words.

STOW	SLOW	STEW	LOW	STOLE
9687	96418	9147	9647	147

Write the correct code for each word.

33 STOW _____ **34** SLOW _____ **35** STEW _____ **36** LOW _____ **37** STOLE _____

5

Underline the word in the brackets which goes best with the words given outside the brackets.

Example word, paragraph, sentence (pen, cap, letter, top, stop)

38 bed, bunk, mattress (drawer, cold, warm, film, pillow)

39 car, lorry, bicycle (train, road, bus, speed, track)

40 sheep, cows, chickens (farm, tractor, shed, pigs, bird)

41 money, cash, notes (cheque, bank, lesson, coins, save)

42 mat, tiles, carpet (curtains, rug, kitchen, sofa, stairs)

5

Fill in the crosswords so that all the given words are included. You have been given one letter as a clue in each crossword.

43

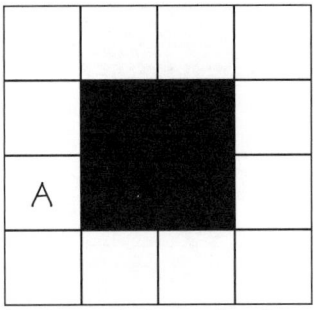

lost, rust, tear, tool

44

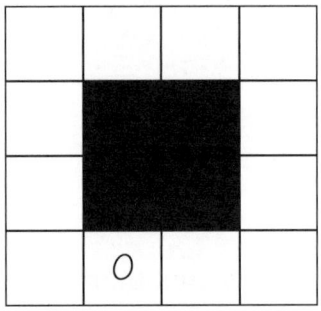

leak, sail, shot, took

45

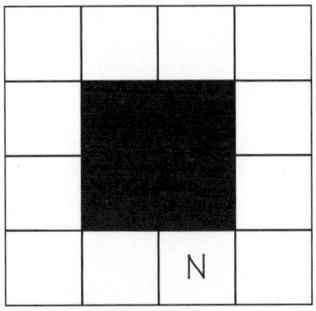

less, list, seek, tank

3

Now go to the Progress Chart to record your score! **Total** 45

Paper 6

Underline one word in the brackets which is most opposite in meaning to the word in capital letters.

Example WIDE (broad vague long <u>narrow</u> motorway)

1 SHORT (length long low metre up)

2 UP (saw went go down tall)

3 YOUNG (old clothes pretty dress new)

4 EVEN (smooth plain old odd straight)

5 FASTEN (collar fix loosen tie bind)

5

Fill in the crosswords so that all the given words are included. You have been given one letter as a clue in each crossword.

6

	R		
	■	■	
	■	■	

even, idle, iron, noon

7

	E		
	■	■	
	■	■	

told, nail, want, went

8

		T	
	■	■	
	■	■	

bare, hare, bath, rear

3

In each line one word has been muddled up. Rearrange the letters so it fits in with the others.

Example fly spider moth gnat tan ant

9 dove lark wren tit low _____

10 rain owns mist hail fog _____

11 lump pear date lime apple _____

12 cake pork wets buns ham _____

13 goat lamb deer loaf calf _____

5

Change the first word into the last word by changing one letter at a time and making a new, different word in the middle.

Example CASE CASH LASH

14 LAND _____ PAID

15 PLAN _____ CLAP

16 PAID _____ HAIL

17 WAND _____ FIND

18 SILK _____ TILL

5

Change the first word of the third pair in the same way as the other pairs to give a new word.

Example bind, hind bare, hare but, hut

19 rest, test road, toad rent, _____

20 chip, hip park, ark mice, _____

21 tear, tar fear, far bear, _____

22 bet, beat set, seat met, _____

23 and, band old, bold all, _____

5

In each line, underline the word that has its letters in alphabetical order.

24 ace debt eight more

25 few lips most room

2

Find the three-letter word which can be added to the letters in capitals to make a new word. The new word will complete the sentence sensibly.

Example The cat sprang onto the MO. USE

26 A donkey BS. _____

27 A cock CS. _____

28 A lion RS. _____

29 A dog BS. _____

30 A pig GTS. _____

5

If the code for LATHER is ABCDEF, what are the codes for the following words?

31 REAL _____ **32** LATE _____ **33** HEAL _____

What do these codes stand for?

34 DEF _____ **35** CEECD _____

5

The day after tomorrow is Friday.

36 What was the day before yesterday? _____

If Joshua was a year older he would be three times as old as his brother. His brother is 4.

37 How old is Joshua? _____

I have 20p more than Gita who has 40p less than Mike. Mike has £1.20.

38 How much does Gita have? _____

39 How much do I have? _____ 4

Underline the two words which are the odd ones out in the following groups of words.

Example	black	<u>king</u>	purple	green	<u>house</u>
40	banana	pear	yellow	purple	apple
41	finger	ring	knee	hat	ear
42	rose	daffodil	daisy	leaf	stem
43	tennis	bat	ball	rugby	swimming

4

Fill in the crosswords so that all the given words are included. You have been given one letter as a clue in each crossword.

44

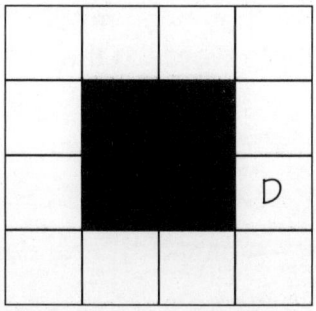

ends, laze, lent, tins

45

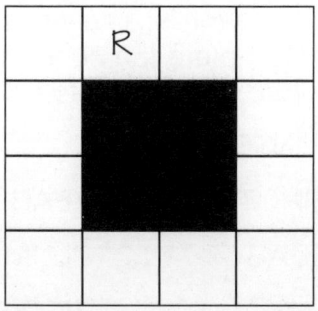

bear, ever, gate, grab

2

Now go to the Progress Chart to record your score! **Total** 45

Paper 7

Look at these groups of words.

Group A Animals Group B Colours Group C Birds

Choose the correct group for each of the words below. Write in the letter.

1 purple ___ **2** ferret ___ **3** swan ___ **4** rabbit ___ **5** wren ___ 5

Underline the pair of words most opposite in meaning.

	Example	cup, mug	coffee, milk	<u>hot, cold</u>
6	yes, no	tall, fat	roam, wander
7	happy, glad	teach, learn	blue, sea
8	sorry, cry	quick, run	less, more
9	work, play	high, jump	bright, shining
10	rain, puddle	cat, food	wet, dry

5

Underline the one word which **cannot be made** from the letters of the word in capital letters.

	Example	STATIONERY	stone	tyres	ration	<u>nation</u>	noisy
11	PROFITS	frost	stiff	spot	soft	sport
12	GROWING	ring	gnaw	grin	wing	iron
13	COWARDS	ward	draws	soars	sword	crow
14	GRAPPLE	pear	rage	leap	gate	grape
15	PATIENT	tape	pint	teen	tent	neat

5

Look at the first group of three words. The word in the middle has been made from the other two words. Complete the second group of three words in the same way, making a new word in the middle.

	Example	PA<u>IN</u>	INTO	<u>TO</u>OK	ALSO	<u>SOON</u>	ONLY
16	CAME	MESH	SHOT	YEAR	_____	CHIN
17	GRIN	GRAB	STAB	PLUM	_____	SCAN
18	MALT	ALSO	SAGO	SMOG	_____	SEAS
19	GATE	GAME	TIME	ROPE	_____	HOSE
20	THIN	MOTH	MOON	STAB	_____	PEGS

5

Complete the following sentences by selecting the most sensible word from each group of words given in the brackets. Underline the words selected.

Example The (children, books, foxes) carried the (houses, books, steps) home from the (greengrocer, library, factory).

21 Tom saw a (bird, walrus, rabbit) run down a (chimney, hole, pavement) and into its (drey, burrow, sleep).

22 I feel (cold, lazy, hot) so I must put on a (swim suit, jumper, sandals) – then I will feel warmer in this chilly (sun, wind, day).

23 The (firework, balloons, streamers) were (burst, inflated, candle) to decorate the (room, table, ladder) for the party.

24 Clare (wrote, played, sent) a (page, text, letter) to Anya's mobile (bike, phone, pencil).

25 They (ran, walked, swam) across the (house, class, lake) to the (mist, frog, island).

5

Remove one letter from the word in capital letters to leave a new word. The meaning of the new word is given in the clue.

Example AUNT an insect ant

26 BLESS fewer _____

27 THEN a chicken _____

28 MEAN male _____

29 REED a colour _____

4

Fill in the crosswords so that all the given words are included. You have been given one letter as a clue in each crossword.

30

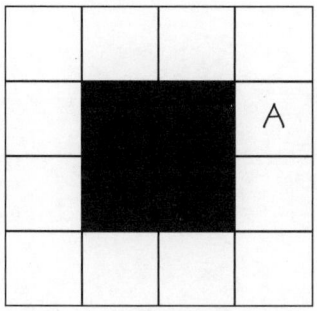

host, hymn, note, take

31

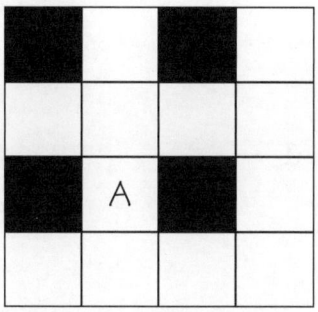

ants, arts, open, spar

2

32 If the code for SPIN is ABDE, what is the code for NIPS? _____

33 If the code for RING is CDEF, what is the code for GRIN? _____

34 If the code for SPRIG is ABCDF, what is the code for PRIG? _____

35 If the code for SEAT is 3521, what is the code for TEAS? _____

36 If the code for STEAM is 31526, what is the code for MAST? _____ 5

Fill in the missing number or letters in each sequence.

Example 2 4 6 8 10

37 10 20 40 __ 160

38 28 24 20 __ 12

39 19 25 __ 37 43

40 11 __ 17 20 23

41 bb bc bd __ bf 5

Look at this chart.

	English	Art	Maths	Science	ICT
Class 1	4	2	4	6	3
Class 2	5	6	2	1	3

42 Which subject is liked by twice as many Class 1 pupils as Class 2 pupils? _____

43 Which subject is three times as popular with Class 2 as with Class 1? _____

44 Which subject is least popular with Class 2? _____ 4

45 Which subject was liked equally well by Class 1 and Class 2? _____

Now go to the Progress Chart to record your score! Total

Paper 8

If a = 1, b = 2, c = 3, d = 4, e = 5, f = 6, find the sum of:

1 a + b + c = __

2 d + e + f = __

3 2a + b = __

4 2b + c = __

5 3a + 2b = __

6 e + f = __ 6

Rearrange the muddled letters in capitals to make a proper word. The answer will complete the sentence sensibly.

Example A BEZAR is an animal with stripes. ZEBRA

7 Half of six is HERET. _____

8 Sheep have a thick OLWO coat. _____

9 Don't drop TILTRE in the street. _____

10 The fire crew used AETRW to put out the blaze. _____

11 The tower of the HRCCHU was floodlit. _____ 5

Complete the following sentences by selecting the most sensible word from each group of words given in the brackets. Underline the words selected.

Example The (children, books, foxes) carried the (houses, books, steps) home from the (greengrocer, library, factory).

12 It was (hot, cold, freezing) and she (hated, wanted, disliked) a (pie, hot soup, cold drink) to cool her down.

13 Where is my (shoe, coat, book)? I left it (hiding, running, hanging) in the (shelf, kitchen, cupboard).

14 The (king, soldier, dog) sat in his (car, basket, larder) and (swam, growled, argued). 3

Underline the pair of words most opposite in meaning.

Example cup, mug coffee, milk hot, cold

15	cross, happy	sad, sorry	start, begin
16	neat, tidy	hard, soft	soap, water
17	eat, drink	boil, water	loud, noisy
18	cold, cool	shut, open	oil, tank
19	paper, pencil	pen, write	cry, laugh

5

Look at the first group of three words. The word in the middle has been made from the other two words. Complete the second group of three words in the same way, making a new word in the middle.

Example PAIN INTO TOOK ALSO SOON ONLY

20	RASH	RAIN	GRIN	CLAN	_____	SLIP
21	POST	STAR	ARMY	POSH	_____	INTO

22	CRAG	CREW	EWES	BLUE	_____	ABLE
23	CHAT	CHIN	RAIN	SLAT	_____	SHAM
24	OVEN	VERY	YOUR	BACK	_____	ETCH

5

Underline the two words which are the odd ones out in the following groups of words.

Example black <u>king</u> purple green <u>house</u>

25	cot	sleep	cradle	sing	bed
26	cat	little	water	minute	small
27	road	long	tall	street	fat
28	coat	new	dress	pretty	suit
29	sorry	pleased	happy	glad	old

5

Fill in the missing letters. The alphabet has been written out to help you.

A B C D E F G H I J K L M N O P Q R S T U V W X Y Z

Example AB is to CD as PQ is to <u>RS</u>.

30 A30 is to B29 as C28 is to _____.

31 D20 is to E19 as F18 is to _____.

32 100A is to 95B as 90C is to _____.

33 A2 is to B3 as C4 is to _____.

34 F1 is to E2 as D3 is to _____.

5

Find and underline the two words which need to change places for each sentence to make sense.

Example She went to <u>letter</u> the <u>write</u>.

35 The drive was parked in the car.

36 We went to holiday for our Scotland.

37 I have to eat my pudding before I can have supper.

38 The shop on my road sweets sells.

39 We are moving our house and selling to Wales.

5

If the code for SECOND is ABCDEF, what are the codes for the following words?

40 ONE _____ **41** CODE _____ **42** ONCE _____

What do these codes stand for?

43 FDEB _____ **44** FDAB _____ **45** ABEF _____ 6

Now go to the Progress Chart to record your score! **Total** 45

Paper 9

Underline the pair of words most similar in meaning.

Example come, go <u>roam, wander</u> fear, fare

1	fade, tint	blank, empty	hinder, go
2	cut, slit	hit, miss	less, more
3	dry, fine	rich, poor	tea, coffee
4	add, subtract	hole, gap	red, colour
5	tired, weary	hot, cold	forgot, remember

5

Find the three-letter word which can be added to the letters in capitals to make a new word. The new word will complete the sentence sensibly.

Example The cat sprang onto the MO. <u>USE</u>

6 The police will FOL the criminal. _____

7 A DON is sometimes called an ass. _____

8 Time to stop for a DR of water. _____

9 He was pleased to go home from HOSAL. _____

10 You need a BET to carry your shopping in. _____ 5

Find the letter which will end the first word and start the second word.

Example peac (<u>h</u>) ome

11 gat (__) nds **12** non (__) ars **13** min (__) ust

14 ben (__) rim **15** als (__) dds 5

Look at the first group of three words. The word in the middle has been made from the other two words. Complete the second group of three words in the same way, making a new word in the middle.

Example	PAIN	INTO	TOOK		ALSO	SOON	ONLY
16	CLAN	CLOP	STOP		RATS	_____	FISH
17	BAND	BARK	DARK		SLIP	_____	GROW
18	FISH	SHOE	WOES		FAST	_____	TOWN
19	SALT	ALSO	SOOT		PART	_____	CHOP
20	BUSH	BUNK	PINK		STEP	_____	SHOP

5

Complete the following sentences by selecting the most sensible word from each group of words given in the brackets. Underline the words selected.

Example The (children, books, foxes) carried the (houses, books, steps) home from the (greengrocer, library, factory).

21 She spent a (lot, little, some) of money on all the things she had to (buy, sell, gather) for the big (party, card, mess).

22 The (dog, cow, rabbit) barked (kindly, fiercely, slowly) at the (burglars, robbing, scare).

23 Tola (buy, bought, bring) her brother a DVD as a (present, surprised, gifts) for (his, her, my) birthday.

24 Don't (run, walk, stand)! You'll (stop, wait, trip) and hurt your (book, friend, knee).

25 The cinema was (dry, packed, fill) for the premiere of the (pictures, movie, showing) with an all-star (sky, moon, cast).

5

If the code for WONDER is 324165, what are the codes for the following words?

26 END _____ **27** DEW _____

What do these codes stand for?

28 324 _____ **29** 3564 _____ **30** 246 _____

5

If a = 1, b = 2, c = 3, d = 4, e = 5, find the sum of:

31 c + d + b = __ **32** 2a + 2 = __ **33** 2c + 2d = __

3

It takes 1 hour 30 minutes to do the journey. Fill in the missing times.

34–37

Southby (depart)	Eastby (arrive)
_____	12:00
14:30	_____
16:10	_____
_____	18:30

4

If the letters in the following words are arranged in alphabetical order, which letter comes in the middle?

38 FAIRY ____ **39** PLACE ____

40 LIGHT ____ **41** TEACH ____

4

Worzles and Dingbats like to eat leaves and shoots.

Sninks and Dingbats like snails and slugs.

Worzles and Wigglers like weeds and grass.

Wigglers and Sninks like flies and berries.

42 Who likes berries but not weeds? _____

43 Who likes leaves, shoots and slugs? _____

44 Who likes snails and flies? _____

45 Who likes weeds, grass, flies and berries? _____

4

Now go to the Progress Chart to record your score! **Total** 45

Paper 10

Underline the two words which are the odd ones out in the following groups of words.

Example black <u>king</u> purple green <u>house</u>

1 child wash clean parent bath

2 circle newspaper ring hoop comic

3	grey	yellow	apple	blue	cherry
4	jeans	turban	white	brown	sweater
5	bench	arm	seat	chair	leg

5

Find the three-letter word which can be added to the letters in capitals to make a new word. The new word will complete the sentence sensibly.

Example The cat sprang onto the MO. USE

6 The CH he sat on was hard. _____

7 The CSE of the river was long and winding. _____

8 The show INS at eight o'clock. _____

9 At the start of the play the ORS appeared on the stage. _____

10 The BN and white dog ran wildly after the ball. _____

5

Find the letter which will end the first word and start the second word.

Example peac (h) ome

11 lan (__) are

12 fea (__) ule

13 gon (__) ver

14 sto (__) ond

15 cla (__) hite

5

These words have been written in code, but the codes are not under the right words.

AT	THE	CHAT	HAT	ACT
2315	15	125	534	315

Write the correct code for each word.

16 AT _____

17 THE _____

18 CHAT _____

19 HAT _____

20 ACT _____

5

Paper 1 (pages 1–3)

1 **alley, lane** Both words mean a type of path or narrow road.
2 **heavy, weighty** Both words mean bulky or big.
3 **bite, nip** Both words mean to snap at or pinch with teeth.
4 **correct, right** Both words mean accurate or exact.
5 **closed, shut** Both words mean fastened or secure.
6 **EVE** seven
7 **HOE** shoes
8 **ILL** filled
9 **HOW** showed
10 **FOR** before
11 **below**
12 **inside**
13 **forgot**
14 **fingertip**
15 **handsome**
16 **pant** The pattern is to put 'p' in front of the first word.
17 **tear** The pattern is to put 't' in front of the first word.
18 **tried** The pattern is to put 'r' after the first letter in the first word.
19 **pain** The pattern is to insert 'i' after the second letter in the first word.
20 **stab** The pattern is to put 's' in front of the first word.
21 **J** The letters move forwards by three letters.
22 **6H** The numbers increase by 1 each time. The letters move forwards by two letters.
23 **DEG** All the letters move forwards by one letter.
24 **PDE** All the letters move forwards by one letter.
25 **6GH** The numbers decrease by 1 each time. All the letters move forwards by two letters.

26

H	O	M	E
I			D
N			I
T	E	N	T

27

T	E	R	M
I			O
M			S
E	N	D	S

28

W	I	S	H
A			E
G			A
S	H	I	P

29 **18** The numbers increase by 3 each time.
30 **2000** The numbers increase by 2 each time.
31 **8** The numbers decrease by 3 each time.
32 **6.5** The numbers increase by 0.5 each time.
33 **20** The number added increases by 1 each time: +1, +2, +3, +4
34 **6** The number subtracted decreases by 1 each time: –2, –3, –4, –5
35 **573** A = 5, R = 7, E = 3
36 **751** R = 7, A = 5, P = 1
37 **915** S = 9, P = 1, A = 5
38 **933** S = 9, E = 3, E = 3
39 **135** P = 1, E = 3, A = 5
40 **SPEAR** 9 = S, 1 = P, 3 = E, 5 = A, 7 = R
41 **APPEAR** 5 = A, 1 = P, 1 = P, 3 = E, 5 = A, 7 = R
42 **15 minutes** From 14:00 to 14:15 is 15 minutes.
43 **75 minutes** From 14:15 to 15:30 is 75 minutes.
44 **30 minutes** From 15:30 to 16:00 is 30 minutes.
45 **30 minutes** From 16:00 to 16:30 is 30 minutes.

Paper 2 (pages 4–7)

1–5 A word that has the same or similar meaning to another word is called a synonym. For example, 'gigantic' is a synonym of 'large'.
1 **bright** 'Clever' and 'bright' are both synonyms meaning intelligent.
2 **fast** 'Quick' and 'fast' are both synonyms meaning speedy.
3 **chuckle** 'Laugh' and 'chuckle' are both sounds showing amusement.
4 **new** 'Modern' and 'new' are both synonyms meaning up to date, fresh.
5 **easy** 'Simple' and 'easy' are both synonyms meaning straightforward.
6–10 Solve these questions by looking at the first set of three and working out how the first and last numbers have been used to arrive at the middle number. Apply this to the second set of three and see if it works. If it does, apply it to the last set.
6 **7** 3 + 6 = 9 and 4 + 2 = 6 so 1 + 6 = 7
7 **12** 5 × 2 = 10 and 4 × 3 = 12 so 6 × 2 = 12
8 **10** 2 + 3 = 5 and 7 + 1 = 8 so 2 + 8 = 10
9 **4** 7 – 1 = 6 and 5 – 2 = 3 so 8 – 4 = 4
10 **4** 15 ÷ 3 = 5 and 21 ÷ 7 = 3 so 16 ÷ 4 = 4
11 **d** hand, door
12 **e** mate, ever
13 **t** salt, till
14 **k** duck, kite
15 **t** mast, test

16

C	A	M	P
A			L
T			U
S	H	A	M

17

B	E	N	D
E			A
A			R
M	I	L	K

18

B	A	N	K
E			I
A			N
R	I	N	G

19 **bedside**
20 **underground**
21 **inform**
22 **outlaw**
23 **forgive**
24 **PINE**
25 **COME**
26 **COPE**
27 **MATE**
28 **GOLD**
29 **5632** S = 5, T = 6, O = 3, P = 2
30 **586** S = 5, E = 8, T = 6
31 **TOP** 6 = T, 3 = O, 2 = P
32 **TOSS** 6 = T, 3 = O, 5 = S, 5 = S
33 **ERR** 8 = E, 9 = R, 9 = R
34 **walls** A 'house' must have 'walls' to be a house. It may or may not have the other things.
35 **water** A 'lake' consists of 'water'. It must have this. It may or may not have the other things.
36 **buildings** A 'city' consists of lots of 'buildings'. It must have these. It may or may not have the other things.
37 **a stove** A 'kitchen' is a place where food is prepared and cooked. Of all the words mentioned, 'a stove' is the word that connects it to a 'kitchen'.
38 **students** A 'school' is where 'students' study. It must have these. It may or may not have the other things.
39 **MEAT, TEAM**
40 **TEN, NET**
41 **LAST, SALT**
42 **far**
43 **ham**
44 **round**
45 **tan**

Paper 3 (pages 7–10)

1 **crowd, concert** All the other words mean tranquil.
2 **enlarge, expand** All the other words mean 'not very long'.
3 **harbour, pier** All the other words are bodies of water.
4 **weak, ill** All the other words mean fit or well.
5 **swim, dive** All the other words are actions you do out of the water.
6 **ARM** warm
7 **EAR** searched
8 **JAM** pyjamas
9 **COT** apricot
10 **TEN** tentacles
11 **p** plate, please, pony, peach
12 **b** bright, big, ball, bean
13 **s** show, set, spoon, snake
14 **m** melt, meal, mat, moan
15 **s** shall, seal, small, snail
16 **trout**
17 **noise**
18 **thick**
19 **plate**
20 **sport**

21

M	I	S	T
A			R
R			I
K	E	E	P

22

H	A	L	F
A			I
R			R
D	A	T	E

23

P	A	R	T
E			I
A			D
R	I	P	E

24 **12** The numbers increase by 3 each time.
25 **6** The numbers decrease by 2 each time.
26 **36** The numbers increase by 12 each time.
27 **54** The numbers increase by 11 each time.
28 **343** The numbers increase by 111 each time.
29–33 Three of the words begin with 'T'. Look at the beginning of the codes. Three of the codes start with '7'. Therefore, 'T' = '7'. From this information, you can deduce TO = 72. 'O' therefore = 2. So, TOO = 722. You can now work out all the other codes.
29 **722** T = 7, O = 2, O = 2
30 **247** O = 2, U = 4, T = 7
31 **727** T = 7, O = 2, T = 7
32 **72** T = 7, O = 2
33 **46** U = 4, P = 6
34 **6** 1 + 2 + 3 = 6
35 **7** 3 + (2 × 2) = 7
36 **6** (2 × 1) + (2 × 2) = 6
37 **dear** There is no 'a' in CONSIDER.
38 **flow** There is no 'f' in LOWEST.
39 **eaten** There is no 'n' in TEACHER.
40 **need** There is only one 'e' in INSIDE.
41–45 Write out the alphabet to help you. Go through each of the words in turn looking at the positioning of the letters.
41 **got**
42 **ant**
43 **cry**
44 **dint**
45 **flow**

Paper 4 (pages 10–13)

1 The **dog** wagged her **tail** when she saw the treat.
2 My **mother** told my **sister** to finish her homework.

3 I like to read a **book** before **bed**.
4 At my birthday **party** we ate ice cream and **cake**.
5 My mum takes the **bus** to her **office**.
6 **seaweed**
7 **sandcastle**
8 **workshop**
9 **handshake**
10 **underwater**
11

P	O	R	T
A			O
R			R
K	E	E	N

12

H	E	A	L
O			A
L			Z
E	A	S	Y

13 **ill** 'Healthy' is well whereas 'ill' is unwell.
14 **pupil** A 'teacher' instructs a 'pupil' so that a pupil learns.
15 **foe** A 'friend' is an ally whereas a 'foe' is an enemy.
16 **few** 'Many' is a lot of something whereas a 'few' means very little.
17 **part** 'Whole' means complete whereas 'part' is a section.
18 **FAN** infant
19 **RAM** pram
20 **RAW** crawls
21 **RAT** rattle
22 **AIR** highchair
23 **wasp**
24 **hope**
25 **slow**
26 **halt**
27 **rain**
28 **pink** 'K' is added to 'pin' to make 'pink' as 'k' has been added to 'sun' to make 'sunk'.
29 **hear** An 'eye' is used to 'see' in the same way an 'ear' is used 'hear'.
30 **lead** 'A' is added to 'led' as the third letter to make 'lead' as 'a' has been added to 'bed' as the third letter to make 'bead'.
31 **left** 'Top' is the opposite to 'bottom 'in the same way 'right' is the opposite of 'left'.
32 **think** 'Speak' means to 'talk' in the same way as 'consider' means to 'think'.
33 **bill** as 'B' is added as the first letter to 'ill' to make 'bill' as 'b' has been added as the first letter to 'ail' to make 'bail'.
34 **she** Arrange the words in a grid to make it easier to put them in the correct alphabetical order:

boy	yob	4th
but	tub	2nd
why	yhw	3rd
she	ehs	1st
sty	yts	5th

35–39 BE must be 24 as it is the only two-lettered word. As 4 = E, you know BEE = 244. From this you can deduce BEG and BIN and therefore BEGIN.
35 **24** B = 2, E = 4
36 **245** B = 2, E = 4, G = 5
37 **238** B = 2, I = 3, N = 8
38 **244** B = 2, E = 4, E = 4
39 **24538** B = 2, E = 4, G = 5, I = 3, N = 8
40 **14** (2 × 10) – (2 × 3) = 14
41 **12** (2 × 8) – (2 × 2) = 12
42–45 Use a grid to help you:

	Yellow top	Red top	Green trousers	Brown trousers
SUE	✓			✓
OMAR	✓		✓	
LEE		✓	✓	
JESS		✓		✓

42 **Sue**
43 **Lee**
44 **Omar**
45 **Jess**

Paper 5 (pages 13–16)

1 **h** harm, hand, has, hollow
2 **c** cold, chill, cloud, can
3 **d** dread, dream, dark, dome
4 **b** band, bright, bear, beach
5 **p** prim, power, pride, plant
6 **11:00** Ten minutes after 10:50 is 11:00 as there are sixty minutes in an hour.
7 **18:35** Twenty minutes added on to 18:15 is 18:35.
8 **12:10** Fifty minutes taken from 13:00 is 12:10 as there are sixty minutes in an hour.
9–12 Use grids to help you find the order.
9 **Friday**

Monday	2nd
Thursday	3rd
Wednesday	5th
Friday	1st
Tuesday	4th

10 **April**

May	5th
January	3rd
March	4th
February	2nd
April	1st

11 **dog**

giraffe	3rd
elephant	2nd
mouse	5th
horse	4th
dog	1st

12 **balloon**

plane	4th
helicopter	2nd
kite	3rd
balloon	1st
rocket	5th

13 **cold** If something is 'warm' it is reasonably hot. The nearest opposite to this is 'cold'.
14 **white** 'Black' is very dark whereas 'white' is very pale or bright.
15 **find** To 'hide' something is to obscure or hold back whereas to 'find' something is to locate or discover it.
16 **less** 'More' is an increase of something whereas 'less' is a decrease of something.
17 **last** 'First' is the initial one whereas 'last' is the final one or at the end.
18 **PART, TRAP**
19 **AGES, SAGE**
20 **LEAP, PEAL**
21 **WARD, DRAW**
22 **LATE, TALE**
23 **rod**
24 **pin**
25 **tin**
26 **cod**
27 **arm**
28 **64** 4 is multiplied by 4 to make 16, so 16 × 4 = 64
29 **48** 3 is multiplied by 4 to make 12, so 12 × 4 = 48
30 **8** 32 is divided by 2 to make 16, so 16 ÷ 2 = 8
31 **12** 55 is divided by 5 to make 11, so 60 ÷ 5 = 12
32 **45** 100 divided by 2 to make 50, so 90 ÷ 2 = 45
33–37 There is only one three-letter word so you know LOW = 147. All the other words begin with S, so you know S = 9. There is only one five-letter word so you know STOLE = 96418. From this information, you can work out all the codes.
33 **9647** S = 9, T = 6, O = 4, W = 7
34 **9147** S = 9, L = 1, O = 4, W = 7
35 **9687** S = 9, T = 6, E = 8, W = 7
36 **147** L = 1, O = 4, W = 7
37 **96418** S = 9, T = 6, O = 4, L = 1, E = 8
38 **pillow** The three words are connected with beds, as is 'pillow'.
39 **bus** The three words are all forms of transport that run on roads, as is 'bus'. (A 'train' runs on rails.)
40 **pigs** The three words are all farm animals, as are 'pigs'.
41 **coins** The three words are all physical forms of money, as are 'coins'.
42 **rug** The three words are all floor coverings, as is 'rug'.

43

T	O	O	L
E			O
A			S
R	U	S	T

44

S	A	I	L
H			E
O			A
T	O	O	K

45

L	E	S	S
I			E
S			E
T	A	N	K

Paper 6 (pages 16–19)

1 **long** 'Short' means brief and 'long' means lengthy.
2 **down** 'Up' is above and 'down' is below.
3 **old** 'Young' is youthful and 'old' is ancient.
4 **odd** 'Even' numbers are 2, 4, 6 and so on whereas 'odd' numbers are 1, 3, 5 and so on.
5 **loosen** 'Fasten' is to tighten or do up whereas 'loosen' is to open up or relax something.

6

I	R	O	N
D			O
L			O
E	V	E	N

7

W	E	N	T
A			O
N	A	I	L
T			D

8

B	A	T	H
A			A
R	E	A	R
E			E

9 **owl** Four of the words are types of bird. The letters of 'low' can be rearranged to make 'owl'.

10 **snow** Four of the words are types of weather. The letters of 'owns' can be rearranged to make 'snow'.
11 **plum** Four of the words are types of fruit. The letters of 'lump' can be rearranged to make 'plum'.
12 **stew** Four of the words are foods. The letters of 'wets' can be rearranged to make 'stew'.
13 **foal** Four of the words are animals. The letters of 'loaf' can be rearranged to make 'foal'.
14 **LAID**
15 **CLAN**
16 **PAIL**
17 **WIND**
18 **SILL**
19 **tent** The pattern is to remove 'r' from the beginning of the first word and replace it with 't'.
20 **ice** The pattern is to remove the first letter of the first word.
21 **bar** The pattern is to remove the second letter of the first word – 'e'.
22 **meat** The pattern is to insert the letter 'a' after the second letter 'e'.
23 **ball** The pattern is to insert the letter 'b' at the front of the first word.
24–25 Write out the alphabet to help you. Go through each of the words in turn looking at the positioning of the letters.
24 **ace**
25 **most**
26 **RAY** brays
27 **ROW** crows
28 **OAR** roars
29 **ARK** barks
30 **RUN** grunts
31 **FEBA** R = F, E = E, A = B, L = A
32 **ABCE** L = A, A = B, T = C, E = E
33 **DEBA** H = D, E = E, A = B, L = A
34 **HER** D = H, E = E, F = R
35 **TEETH** C = T, E = E, E = E, C = T, D = H
36 **Monday**

Monday	Day before yesterday
Tuesday	Yesterday
Wednesday	Today
Thursday	Tomorrow
Friday	Day after tomorrow

37 **11** If the brother is 4, three times his age would be 12. Joshua's age is therefore 11 as he is a year short of being three times his brother's age.
38–39 If Mike has £1.20, Gita has 40p less, therefore 80p. I must have £1 as I have 20p more than Gita.
38 **80p**
39 **£1.00**
40 **yellow, purple** The other words are fruit.
41 **ring, hat** The other words are parts of the body.
42 **leaf, stem** The other words are types of flower.
43 **bat, ball** The other words are sports.

44

L	A	Z	E
E			N
N			D
T	I	N	S

45

G	R	A	B
A			E
T			A
E	V	E	R

Paper 7 (pages 20–22)

1–5 Category A Animals (**ferret, rabbit**)
Category B Colours (**purple**)
Category C Birds (**swan, wren**)
6 **yes, no** 'Yes' means to agree or assent whereas 'no' means to disagree or dissent.
7 **teach, learn** 'Teach' is to impart knowledge whereas 'learn' is to gain it.
8 **less, more** 'Less' is fewer whereas 'more' is an increased amount.
9 **work, play** 'Work' is to study or labour whereas 'play' is to relax or to be at leisure.
10 **wet, dry** 'Wet' is filled with water whereas 'dry' is without water.
11 **stiff** There is only one 'f' in PROFITS.
12 **gnaw** There is no 'a' in GROWING.
13 **soars** There is only one 's' in COWARDS.
14 **gate** There is no 't' in GRAPPLE.
15 **teen** There is only one 'e' in PATIENT.
16 **ARCH**

	1	2	
C	A	M	E

3	4		
s	H	O	T

		1	2
Y	E	A	R

3	4		
C	H	I	N

17 **PLAN**

1	2		
G	R	I	N

		3	4
S	T	A	B

1	2		
P	L	U	M

		3	4
S	C	A	N

18 **MOSS**

	1?	2	
M	A	L	T

3	1?		4
S	A	G	O

	1?	2	
S	M	O	G

3	1?		4
S	E	A	S

19 **ROSE**

1	2		4?
G	A	T	E

		3	4?
T	I	M	E

1	2		4?
R	O	P	E

		3	4?
H	O	S	E

20 **PEST**

3	4		
T	H	I	N

1	2?	2?	
M	O	O	N

3	4		
S	T	A	B

1	2?	2?	
P	E	G	S

21–25 Try each of the words in the first set of brackets. Do they make sense with any words in the second and third set of brackets? Only one combination of three words makes sense.

21 **rabbit, hole, burrow**
22 **cold, jumper, wind**
23 **balloons, inflated, room**
24 **sent, text, phone**
25 **swam, lake, island**
26 **less**
27 **hen**
28 **man**
29 **red**
30

H	O	S	T
Y			A
M			K
N	O	T	E

31

	S		A
O	P	E	N
	A		T
A	R	T	S

32 **EDBA** N = E, I = D, P = B, S = A
33 **FCDE** G = F, R = C, I = D, N = E
34 **BCDF** P = B, R = C, I = D, G = F
35 **1523** T = 1, E = 5, A = 2, S = 3
36 **6231** M = 6, A = 2, S = 3, T = 1
37 **80** The numbers double each time.
38 **16** The numbers decrease by 4 each time.
39 **31** The numbers increase by 6 each time.
40 **14** The numbers increase by 3 each time.
41 **be** The first letter is always 'b'. The second letter moves forward one place.
42 **Maths** 4 Class 1 pupils like Maths, which is twice the number of Class 2 pupils (2).
43 **Art** 6 Class 2 pupils like Art, which is three times the number of Class 1 pupils (2).
44 **Science** Only 1 Class 2 pupil likes Science.
45 **ICT** The column that has the same number (3) for both Class 1 and Class 2 is ICT.

Paper 8 (pages 22–25)

1 **6** 1 + 2 + 3 = 6
2 **15** 4 + 5 + 6 = 15
3 **4** (2 × 1) + 2 = 4
4 **7** (2 × 2) + 3 = 7
5 **7** (3 × 1) + (2 × 2) = 7
6 **11** 5 + 6 = 11
7 **THREE**
8 **WOOL**
9 **LITTER**
10 **WATER**
11 **CHURCH**

12–14 Try each of the words in the first set of brackets. Do they make sense with any words in the second and third set of brackets? Only one combination of three words makes sense.

12 **hot, wanted, cold drink**
13 **coat, hanging, cupboard**
14 **dog, basket, growled**
15 **cross, happy** 'Cross' means angry whereas 'happy' means joyful.
16 **hard, soft** 'Hard' means solid whereas 'soft' means spongy.
17 **eat, drink** 'Eat' is to consume solid food whereas 'drink' is to swallow a liquid.
18 **shut, open** 'Shut' means closed whereas 'open' means ajar.
19 **cry, laugh** To 'cry' is to express sadness whereas to 'laugh' is to express happiness.
20 **CLIP**

1	2		
R	A	S	H

		3	4
G	R	I	N

1	2		
C	L	A	N

		3	4
S	L	I	P

21 **SHIN**

		1	2
P	O	S	T

3	4		
A	R	M	Y

		1	2
P	O	S	H

3	4		
I	N	T	O

22 **BLAB**

1	2		
C	R	A	G

3	4		
E	W	E	S

1	2		
B	L	U	E

3	4		
A	B	L	E

23 **SLAM**

1	2		
C	H	A	T

		3	4
R	A	I	N

1	2		
S	L	A	T

		3	4
S	H	A	M

24 **ACHE**

	1	2	
O	V	E	N

4			3
Y	O	U	R

	1	2	
B	A	C	K

4			3
E	T	C	H

25 **sleep, sing** The other words are types of beds.
26 **cat, water** The other words all mean tiny.
27 **road, street** These words are nouns, while the others are adjectives (describing words).
28 **new, pretty** The other words are all types of clothing.
29 **sorry, old** The other words all express pleasure.
30 **D27** The letters move forwards one place. The numbers decrease by 1 each time.
31 **G17** The letters move forwards one place. The numbers decrease by 1 each time.
32 **85D** The numbers decrease by 5 each time. The letters move forwards one place.
33 **D5** The letters move forwards one place. The numbers increase by 1 each time.
34 **C4** The letters move backwards one place. The numbers increase by 1 each time.
35 The **car** was parked in the **drive**.
36 We went to **Scotland** for our **holiday**.
37 I have to eat my **supper** before I can have **pudding**.
38 The shop on my road **sells sweets**.
39 We are **selling** our house and **moving** to Wales.
40 **DEB** O = D, N = E, E = B
41 **CDFB** C = C, O = D, D = F, E = B
42 **DECB** O = D, N = E, C = C, E =B
43 **DONE** F = D, D = O, E = N, B = E
44 **DOSE** F = D, D = O, A = S, B = E
45 **SEND** A = S, B = E, E = N, F = D

Paper 9 (pages 25–27)

1 **blank, empty** Both words mean vacant.
2 **cut, slit** Both words mean a gash or a tear.
3 **dry, fine** Both words mean fair weather.
4 **hole, gap** Both words mean a break or an aperture.
5 **tired, weary** Both words mean exhausted.
6 **LOW** follow
7 **KEY** donkey
8 **INK** drink
9 **PIT** hospital
10 **ASK** basket
11 **e** gate, ends
12 **e** none, ears
13 **d** mind, dust
14 **t** bent, trim
15 **o** also, odds
16 **RASH**

1	2		
C	L	A	N

		3	4
S	T	O	P

1	2		
R	A	T	S

		3	4
F	I	S	H

17 **SLOW**

1	2		
B	A	N	D

		3	4
D	A	R	K

1	2		
S	L	I	P

		3	4
G	R	O	W

18 **STOW**

		1	2
F	I	S	H

	3	4	
W	O	E	S

		1	2
F	A	S	T

	3	4	
T	O	W	N

19 **ARCH**

	1	2	
S	A	L	T

3	4		
S	O	O	T

	1	2	
P	A	R	T

3	4		
C	H	O	P

20 **STOP**

1	2		
B	U	S	H

		3	4
P	I	N	K

1	2		
S	T	E	P

		3	4
S	H	O	P

21–25 Try each of the words in the first set of brackets. Do they make sense with any words in the second and third set of brackets? Only one combination of three words makes sense.
21 **lot, buy, party**
22 **dog, fiercely, burglars**
23 **bought, present, his**
24 **run, trip, knee**
25 **packed, movie, cast**
26 **641** E = 6, N = 4, D = 1
27 **163** D = 1, E = 6, W = 3
28 **WON** 3 = W, 2 = O, 4 = N
29 **WREN** 3 = W, 5 = R, 6 = E, 4 = N
30 **ONE** 2 = O, 4 = N, 6 = E

31 **9** 3 + 4 + 2 = 9 32 **4** (2 × 1) + 2 = 4
33 **14** (2 × 3) + (2 × 4) = 14
34–37 **Southby depart 10:30** 1 hour and 30 minutes before midday is 10:30.
Eastby arrive 16:00 1 hour and 30 minutes added to 14:30 is 16:00.
Eastby arrive 17:40 1 hour and 30 minutes added to 16:10 is 17:40.
Southby depart 17:00 1 hour and 30 minutes before 18:30 is 17:00.
38–41 Use a grid to help you:

FAIRY	A	F	**I**	R	Y
PLACE	A	C	**E**	L	P
LIGHT	G	H	**I**	L	T
TEACH	A	C	**E**	H	T

38 **I** 39 **E**
40 **I** 41 **E**
42–45 Use a table to help you:

	Leaves & shoots	Snails & slugs	Weeds & grass	Flies & berries
Worzels	✓		✓	
Dingbats	✓	✓		
Sninks		✓		✓
Wigglers			✓	✓

42 **Sninks** 43 **Dingbats**
44 **Sninks** 45 **Wigglers**

Paper 10 (pages 27–30)

1 **child, parent** The other words are all connected to cleanliness.
2 **newspaper, comic** The other words are all circular objects.
3 **apple, cherry** The other words are all colours.
4 **white, brown** The other words are items of clothing.
5 **arm, leg** The other words are all pieces of furniture you sit on.
6 **AIR** chair 7 **OUR** course
8 **BEG** begins 9 **ACT** actors
10 **ROW** brown
11 **d** land, dare 12 **r** fear, rule
13 **e** gone, ever 14 **p** stop, pond
15 **w** claw, white
16–20 There is only one two-letter word so AT must be 15. There is only one four-letter word so CHAT must be 2315. HAT must be 315, as CHAT is 2315. C is therefore 2 so ACT = 125, leaving THE as 534.
16 **15** 17 **534**
18 **2315** 19 **315**
20 **125**

21 Use a grid to help you:

f	o	u	r	5th
f	o	r	k	4th
f	i	r	e	3rd
f	a	l	l	1st
f	e	e	l	2nd

21 **fork**
22 **E** CHASE in alphabetical order is ACEHS. The middle letter is 'E'.
23–27 Try each of the words in the first set of brackets. Do they make sense with any words in the second and third set of brackets? Only one combination of three words makes sense.
23 **spade, beach, castle**
24 **fixed, pipe, basin**
25 **heard, burglar, house**
26 **help, lift, table**
27 **owl, hooted, wood**
28 **w** whale, wrap, win, wart
29 **b** blame, bright, bone, burn
30 **f** flint, fray, frank, flea
31 **o** open, oat, opal, orange
32 **c** clip, climb, cheat, charm
33 **SORT**

1	2		
V	E	S	T

		3	4
P	A	I	N

1	2		
S	O	M	E

		3	4
T	A	R	T

34 **BULK**

	2	3	
H	A	R	P

1			4
P	O	R	T

	2	3	
G	U	L	P

1			4
B	A	R	K

35 **STAB**

		1	2
M	A	S	H

		3	4
T	R	I	P

		1	2
F	I	S	T

		3	4
G	R	A	B

36 **HOPE**

1	2		
S	E	L	L

		3	4
B	E	A	T

1	2		
H	O	M	E

		3	4
R	I	P	E

37 **EASY**

	1	2	
M	A	R	K

		3	4
H	E	M	S

	1	2	
P	E	A	L

		3	4
B	U	S	Y

38 **loud**
39 **cub**
40 **shin**
41 **lie**
42 **pan**
43 **slip** lips
44 **tools** stool
45 **toga** goat

Paper 11 (pages 31–33)

1

D		L	
O	P	A	L
N		T	
E	V	E	R

2

	H		N
T	A	M	E
	T		E
U	S	E	D

3

C	A	F	E
A		I	
R	U	S	H
T		H	

4–8 Try each of the words in the first set of brackets. Do they make sense with any words in the second and third set of brackets? Only one combination of three words makes sense.
4 **yawned, tired, bed**
5 **bike, swerved, road**
6 **climbed, window, castle**
7 **turned, lights, dark**
8 **danced, rhythm, music**
9 **hairdresser, dentist** I had a toothache so my mother took me to the dentist.
10 **cage, pool** The swimming pool in my town has two diving boards.
11 **newspaper, dictionary** When I asked my mum what a word meant she told me to look it up in the dictionary.
12 **rice, bread** For lunch I like a cheese sandwich on brown bread and an apple.
13 **candle, cake** My birthday cake this year is going to be chocolate sponge.
14 **KEGCK** T = K, R = E, E = G, A = C, T = K
15 **KGCE** T = K, E = G, A = C, R = E
16 **ACI** P = A, A = C, N = I
17 **IGCK** N = I, E = G, A = C, T = K
18 **TRAP** K = T, E = R, C = A, A = P
19 **REAP** E = R, G = E, C = A, A = P
20 **PART** A = P, C = A, E = R, K = T
21 **mist** The pattern is to remove 'l' from the beginning of the first word and replace it with 'm'.
22 **all** The pattern is to remove the first letter from the first word.
23 **rake** The pattern is to remove 'b' from the beginning of the first word and replace it with 'r'.
24 **boat** The pattern is to add 'b' to the front of the first word.
25 **burden, load** Both words mean an object that is carried.
26 **kind, thoughtful** Both words mean considerate or caring.
27 **expect, hope** Both words mean suppose or anticipate.
28 **little, small** Both words mean tiny.
29 **hide, conceal** Both words mean keep away from view or cover.
30 **SHE** shed
31 **RAN** orange
32 **KIN** skin
33 **AGE** pages
34 **HIT** white
35 **e** lone, eggs
36 **h** bath, horn
37 **k** mark, knit
38 **e** pane, else
39 **e** mare, eels
40 **in** inside, increase, indoor, inland
41 **be** because, behind, beneath, become
42 **sea** seaside, seashell, seagull, seabed
43 **out** outside, outstanding, outshine, outright
44 **sand** sandcastle, sandpit, sandstorm, sandpaper
45 **air** airport, airbag, airship, aircraft

Paper 12 (pages 34–36)

1–5 Group A Tools: **axe, saw, hammer**
Group B Musical Instruments: **drum, guitar, piano**
Group C Sports or Games: **cricket, football**
Group D Vegetables: **peas, potatoes**
6 **w** blow, wish
7 **s** pass, spin
8 **w** show, wind
9 **t** must, tidy
10 **f** puff, feed
11 **outfit**
12 **beside**
13 **farewell**
14 **afterwards**
15 **checkout**
16 **boy** 'Boy' is the male equivalent of 'girl' as 'uncle' is the male equivalent of 'aunt'.
17 **doctors** 'Doctors' treat 'patients' in the same way 'teachers' teach 'pupils'.
18 **calf** A 'calf' is a young 'cow' as a 'puppy' is a young 'dog'.
19 **sheep** A 'flock' is a collective noun for a group of 'sheep' as a 'crowd' is a collective noun for a group of 'people'.

20 **burrow** A 'rabbit' lives in a 'burrow' as a 'pig' lives in a 'sty'.

21

S	■	S	■
N	E	W	S
A	■	A	■
G	O	N	E

22

■	R	■	A
H	E	L	D
■	A	■	D
A	P	E	S

23

C	A	S	T
H	■	H	■
E	V	E	N
W	■	D	■

24 **G** Remove A, B, C, D and E. The first letter is 'F', the second is 'G'.

25 **21** There are 26 letters in the alphabet. 26 – 5 = 21

26 **February** 'F' is the sixth letter of the alphabet, so February.

27 **December** 'D' is the fourth letter of the alphabet, so December.

28 **@ ÷ +** W = @, A = ÷, S = +

29 **× ÷ @** R = ×, A = ÷, W = @

30 **– ÷ ×** T = –, A = ÷, R = ×

31 **WAR** @ = W, ÷ = A, × = R

32 **STAR** + = S, – = T, ÷ = A, × = R

33–35

Mr Young's age	27	**30**	35
Joshua's age	**2**	5	**10**

33 **Mr Young's age: 30** Mr Young is 25 years older than Joshua. If Joshua is 5, Mr Young would be 30 (25 + 5).

34 **Joshua's age: 2** If Mr Young was 25 when Joshua was born, two years later Joshua would be two and Mr Young, 27.

35 **Joshua's age: 10** Mr Young is 25 years older than Joshua. If Mr Young is 35, Joshua will be 10 (35 – 25).

36–40 Try each of the words in the first set of brackets. Do they make sense with any words in the second and third set of brackets? Only one combination of three words makes sense.

36 **race, teacher, whistle**

37 **birds, seed, garden**

38 **flowers, pot, door**

39 **table, forks, knives**

40 **cars, work, morning**

41 It is too **cold** to go **outside** today.

42 The fruit **salad** was made with grapes, pear and **apple**.

43 My aunt and uncle come and spend every **Christmas holiday** with us.

44 The police officer told the man to move his **car** because it was blocking the **road**.

45 Sometimes when I look out of my **window** at night I can see the **moon**.

Paper 13 (pages 37–39)

1

S	■	C	■
P	E	A	S
I	■	L	■
T	I	M	E

2

■	T	■	H
T	A	L	E
■	I	■	R
A	L	S	O

3

G	I	R	L
A	■	U	■
T	I	D	Y
E	■	E	■

4 **unhappy, sad** Both words mean miserable.

5 **sharp, pointed** Both words mean having a sharp point.

6 **loud, noisy** Both words mean deafening.

7 **cheap, inexpensive** Both words mean not costing a lot.

8 **terror, fear** Both words mean panic.

9 **sad** 'Cheerful' means happy whereas 'sad' means miserable.

10 **starve** 'Eat' means to feed whereas 'starve' is to go without food.

11 **still** 'Moving' is changing position whereas being 'still' is remaining motionless.

12 **dirty** 'Clean' is spotless whereas 'dirty' is unwashed and unclean.

13 **hinder** 'Help' is to assist whereas 'hinder' is to prevent something from happening.

14 **O** POUND = DNOPU, so 'O' is the middle letter.

15 **N** TRAIN = AINRT, so 'N' is the middle letter.

16 **E** READS = ADERS, so 'E' is the middle letter.

17 **F** AFTER = AEFRT, so 'F' is the middle letter.

18 **rear**

19 **sore**

20 **late**

21 **tale**

22 **sing** 23 **ride**
24 **6413** N = 6, O = 4, S = 1, E = 3
25 **1563** S = 1, A = 5, N = 6, E = 3
26 **463** O = 4, N = 6, E = 3,
27 **NOON** 6 = N, 4 =O, 4 = O, 6 = N
28 **SOON** 1 = S, 4 = O, 4 = O, 6 = N
29–31 Draw a chart to help you.

1	2	3	4	5	6	7	8	9	10
21	22	23	24	25	26	27	28	29	30

11	12	13	14	15	16	17	18	19	20
31	32	33	34	35	36	37	38	39	40

Alteratively use number logic: if 1 is opposite 21, then 2 is opposite 22, and so on. Therefore to find out the 'opposite' of any number, either add or subtract 20.

29 **28** 8 + 20 = 28
30 **34** 14 + 20 = 34
31 **19** 39 – 20 = 19
32 **fear** There is no 'a' in FLOWERS.
33 **need** There is only one 'e' in WANDER.
34 **rote** There is no 'o' in CURATE.
35 **none** There is no 'o' in MEANING.
36 **star** There is no 'r' in FASTEN.
37 **hair** hairpin, hairnet, hairslide, hairdryer
38 **under** undergo, underhand, undermine, underrate
39 **ship** shipmate, shipyard, shipowner, shipshape
40 **up** uproar, upset, upright, upward
41 **cart** cartwheel, cartload, cartridge, carthorse
42–45 Use a chart to help you:

	Green door	Brown windows	Blue windows	Red door
House 1	✓		✓	
House 2	✓	✓		
House 3		✓		✓
House 4			✓	✓

42 1 43 3
44 2 45 4

Paper 14 (pages 40–42)

1 **PINK** 2 **GREY**
3 **NAVY** 4 **MAUVE**
5 **BROWN** 6 **hotplate**
7 **rainbow** 8 **toothache**
9 **football** 10 **fireplace**
11 **moist** 12 **flower**
13 **front** 14 **trots**
15 **ground**
16 **go, come** 'Go' means to move away whereas 'come' means to move towards you.
17 **night, day** 'Night' is when it is dark whereas 'day' is when it is light.
18 **full, empty** 'Full' means replete whereas 'empty' means with nothing in it.
19 **tall, short** 'Tall' means high or lofty whereas 'short' is small or lacking in height.
20 **play, work** 'Play' is recreation whereas 'work' is labour.
21

A		S	
S	E	A	T
K		G	
S	P	O	T

22

	C		H
H	O	P	E
	O		A
S	P	A	R

23

C	H	I	P
A		R	
R	O	O	T
T		N	

24 **CG** Both letters move forwards one place.
25 **8H** The numbers increase by 1 each time. The letters move forwards one place.
26 **WE** The first letters move backwards one place. The second letters move forwards one place.
27 **4S** The numbers increase by 2 each time. The letters move backwards one place.
28 **JP** The first letters move forwards one place. The second letters move backwards one place.
29 **÷ % – +** T = ÷, E = %, A = –, M = +
30 **+ % ÷** M = +, E = %, T = ÷
31 **× % ÷** S = ×, E = %, T = ÷
32 **MAST** + = M, – = A, × = S, ÷ = T
33 **ARMS** – = A, @ = R, + = M, × = S
34 **d** (8 + 7) ÷ 3 = 5; 5 = d
35 **g** 2 + (9 – 3) = 8; 8 = g
36 **b** (4 × 6) ÷ 8 = 3; 3 = b
37–40 Use a chart to help you:

	Mike	Sally	Annie	Kim
Monday	✓	✓	✓	
Tuesday				
Wednesday	✓		✓	✓
Thursday		✓	✓	✓
Friday				
Saturday	✓	✗		✓

37 **none** 38 **Annie**

39 **Kim** 40 **Thursday**

41 **tired, exhausted** Both words mean fatigued or weary.

42 **swerve, dodge** Both words mean to avoid or to run round something.

43 **mean, stingy** Both words mean miserly or penny-pinching.

44 **soldiers, troops** Both words mean military personnel.

45 **double, twice** Both words mean twofold.

Paper 15 (pages 43–45)

1 **grass, lawn** The other words are colours.

2 **wash, dry** The other words mean friend.

3 **house, cottage** The other words are fish.

4 **plate, dish** The other words are types of food.

5 **glove, hat** The other words are all worn on the foot.

6 **light** 7 **wing** 8 **cure**

9 **cat** 10 **hat**

11

S		R	
H	E	A	T
I		I	
P	O	N	Y

12

	F		A
F	E	A	R
	T		M
V	E	R	Y

13

W	I	L	L
I		A	
D	O	T	E
E		E	

14 **sip** The pattern is to remove the second letter of the first word.

15 **feat** The pattern is to insert 'e' after the first letter of the first word.

16 **wets** The pattern is to run the letters of the first word in reverse order.

17 **race** The pattern to swap over the first and third letters of the first word.

18 **flat** The pattern is to remove the letter 'i' from the first word and replace it with 'a'.

19 **6** $1 \times 2 \times 3 = 6$ 20 **7** $(2 \times 4) - 1 = 7$

21 **12** $3 \times 4 = 12$

22–26 Try each of the words in the first set of brackets. Do they make sense with any words in the second and third set of brackets? Only one combination of three words makes sense.

22 **birthday, mother, cake**

23 **eat, chips, fish**

24 **night, wet, windy**

25 **eat, cake, poisoned**

26 **people, seen, city**

27 **+ – – +** P = +, O = –, O = –, P = +

28 **÷ / × –** I = ÷, N = /, T = ×, O = –

29 **– + × ÷ – /** O = –, P = +, T = ×, I = ÷, O = –, N = /

30 **ONION** – = O, / = N, ÷ = I, – = O, / = N

31 **TINT** × = T, ÷ = I, / = N, × = T

32 **hold** 'Contain' and 'hold' both mean to have or to enclose.

33 **final** Something that is 'last' or 'final' comes at the end or the finish.

34 **rich** 'Wealthy' and 'rich' both mean affluent or well-off.

35 **stake** 'Post' and 'stake' both mean a pole or stick.

36 **near, far** 'Near' is close whereas 'far' is a long way away.

37 **save, spend** 'Save' is to keep whereas 'spend' is to use up.

38 **ugly, pretty** 'Ugly' is unattractive whereas 'pretty' is attractive.

39 **friend, enemy** A 'friend' is an ally whereas an 'enemy' is a foe.

40 **quiet, noisy** 'Quiet' is peaceful whereas 'noisy' is loud.

41 We went to the **sea** for our holiday this **year**.

42 Mike likes to go to his grandmother's **house** after **school**.

43 I forgot that **I had** checked a book out of the library.

44 It is important to look **both ways** when crossing the street.

45 I planted some **flowers** in the garden that I'd grown from **seeds**.

Paper 16 (pages 46–48)

1–5 Try each of the words in the first set of brackets. Do they make sense with any words in the second and third set of brackets? Only one combination of three words makes sense.

1 **tired, she, sit**

2 **sister, dance, boyfriend**

3 **left, purse, shop**

4 **ring, ambulance, mobile**

5 **supper, moon, sky**

6 **trees** A 'forest' is a large group of trees so it must have 'trees'.

7 **a tail** It may have all the features but all pigs have 'tails'.

8 **man** A 'husband' is a male partner so must be a 'man'.

9 **with patients** A 'nurse's' job is to look after 'patients'.

10 **Pages** It may have all the features but all books have pages.
11 **December** 12 **eleven**
13 **individual** 14 **release**
15 **alabaster**
16 **+ − × ÷ /** P = +, L = −, E = ×, A = ÷, D = /
17 **÷ + + − ×** A = ÷, P = +, P = +, L = −, E = ×
18 **+ ÷ − ×** P = +, A = ÷, L = −, E = ×
19 **DALE** / = D, ÷ = A, − = L, × = E
20 **DEED** / = D, × = E, × = E, / = D
21 **crate** 22 **sold** 23 **hole**
24 **hard** 25 **super**
26 **children** 'Pupils' are usually young people who learn therefore the closest here is 'children'.
27 **pens** 'Felt tips' are a type of 'pen'.
28 **noises** 'Sounds' can be loud or soft so 'noises' is the best match here.
29 **bungalow** Although some of the words can mean places to live, a 'house' is the most similar to 'bungalow'.
30 **box** Although 'suitcase' and 'crate' are also containers, they are usually used for transporting items. 'Box' is the most similar to 'chest' here as both are used for storing items.
31 **beginning, end** 'Beginning' is the start of something whereas 'end' is the finish.
32 **open, closed** 'Open' means the contents are exposed or accessible whereas 'closed' means the contents are hidden from view or shut away.
33 **high, low** 'High' is up in the air whereas 'low' is close to the ground.
34 **strong, weak** 'Strong' is healthy and sturdy whereas 'weak' is feeble.
35 **quiet, loud** 'Quiet' means making little or no sound whereas 'loud' means making a strong and invasive sound.
36 **END** friends 37 **NUT** minutes
38 **ODE** modern 39 **EAR** years
40 **WAR** reward
41–45 Write out the first six letters to help you: ABCDEF.
41 **feed** 42 **face** 43 **bead**
44 **fade** 45 **add**

Paper 17 (pages 48–50)

1 **3** The Costa Brava has 10 hours of sunshine in July whereas London has 7, so 10 − 7 = 3.
2 **41** 6 + 7 + 7 + 7 + 6 + 5 + 3 = 41 hours
3 **8** 8 + 8 + 9 + 10 + 9 + 7 + 5 = 56. 56 ÷ 7 months = 8
4 **2** The Costa del Sol has 10 hours of sunshine in May whereas the Costa Brava has 8, so 10 − 8 = 2.
5 **13** The Costa del Sol has 11 + 11 + 11 = 33 hours of sunshine. London has 7 + 7 + 6 = 20 hours of sunshine. 33 − 20 = 13 hours difference.
6 **heavy, light** 'Heavy' means weighty whereas 'light' is weightless.
7 **here, there** 'Here' means next to you whereas 'there' indicates a distance away.
8 **whisper, shout** 'Whisper' is to speak very quietly whereas 'shout' is to speak very loud.
9 **late, early** 'Late' is delayed whereas 'early' is ahead of time.
10 **glad, sad** 'Glad' is happy whereas 'sad' is miserable.
11 **ACE** raced 12 **ROT** parrot
13 **TON** buttons 14 **ROW** brown
15 **JOY** enjoys
16 **d** hand, deal 17 **e** mate, ends
18 **t** salt, two 19 **k** duck, know
20 **t** mast, track
21 **NEST**

		1	2	3	4		
H	O	M	E	A	N	T	S

		1	2	3	4		
S	A	N	E	S	T	A	Y

22 **CHIN**

		1	2	3	4		
G	R	E	Y	E	S	P	Y

		1	2	3	4		
E	A	C	H	I	N	C	H

23 **BASH**

1	2			3	4		
W	E	S	T	A	R	T	S

1	2			3	4		
B	A	T	H	S	H	E	D

24 **BEAT**

1			4		2	3	
L	A	R	K	S	I	N	G

1			4		2	3	
B	E	S	T	N	E	A	R

25 **BEST**

1	2			3	4		
F	I	R	E	S	H	O	P

1	2			3	4		
B	E	A	R	S	T	E	W

26 **help, aid** Both the words mean to lend a hand or facilitate.
27 **ruin, spoil** Both the words mean to mar or damage.

28 **angry, cross** Both the words mean enraged or annoyed.
29 **hear, listen** Both the words mean to pay attention to a sound.
30 **price, cost** Both the words mean the amount you have to pay for something.
31–35 Solve these questions by looking at the first set of three and working out how the first and last numbers have been used to arrive at the middle number. Apply this to the second set of three and see if it works. If it does, apply it to the last set.
31 **5** 3 × 3 = 9 and 4 × 2 = 8, so 5 × 1 = 5
32 **9** 4 + 1 = 5 and 2 + 5 = 7, so 6 + 3 = 9
33 **4** 17 – 14 = 3 and 8 – 5 = 3, so 11 – 7 = 4
34 **8** 9 + 3 = 12 and 5 + 7 = 12, so 6 + 2 = 8
35 **3** 30 ÷ 5 = 6 and 18 ÷ 3 = 6, so 24 ÷ 8 = 3
36 **49** 6 × 6 = 36 so 7 × 7 = 49
37 **30** 9 is three quarters of 12 in the same way 30 is three quarters of 40.
38 **28** 14 + 7 = 21 in the same way 21 + 7 = 28.
39 **250** 4 × 5 = 20 in the same way 50 × 5 = 250.
40 **76** 19 × 2 = 38 in the same way 38 × 2 = 76.
41 **seed** Both words mean the part of a plant that will grow into new plants.
42 **icy** Both words mean covered by frozen water.
43 **slide** Both words mean to slip on a surface.
44 **lift** Both words mean to elevate.
45 **tilt** Both words mean to slant or be at an angle.

Paper 18 (pages 51–53)

1–5 Group A Kitchen things: **whisk, scales, recipe**
Group B Languages: **Dutch, German, French**
Group C Birds: **gull, goose**
Group D Animals: **camel, lamb**

6 **ATE** water
7 **CAR** scarf
8 **ARE** share
9 **WAS** washing
10 **TEA** steal
11 **d** land, down
12 **t** feat, turn
13 **g** gong, glass
14 **p** stop, place
15 **e** rope, ear

16

E		S	
Y	E	L	L
E		O	
S	I	P	S

17

F	O	O	D
L		A	
A	C	T	S
G		S	

18 **seat** The pattern is to add 's' to the beginning of the first word.
19 **list** The pattern is to add 's' after the second letter and before the 't'.
20 **moat** The pattern is to add 'o' after the first letter and before the 'a'.
21 **heat** The pattern is to add 'e' after the first letter and before the 'a'.
22 **than** The pattern is to add 'th' to the beginning of the first word.
23 **– / ×** G = –, E = /, T = ×
24 **$ = / @ ×** B = $, L = =, E = /, A = @, T = ×
25 **= / @ + /** L = =, E = /, A = @, V = +, E = /
26 **TAG** × = T, @ = A, – = G,
27 **GATE** – = G, @ = A, × = T, / = E,
28–31 Use a grid to help you:

	Blue jeans	Red shirt	Green shirt	Black jeans
A	✓		✓	
B	✓	✓		
C		✓		✓
D			✓	✓

28 **B**
29 **D**
30 **A**
31 **C**
32 **bead** ABCDEF are the first six letters. 'Bead' is the only word that can be made using only these letters.
33 **E** CRIED = CDEIR. 'E' is the middle letter.
34 **K** BROKE = BEKOR. 'K' is the middle letter.
35 **S** SWEPT = EPSTW. 'S' is the middle letter.
36–40 Try each of the words in the first set of brackets. Do they make sense with any words in the second and third set of brackets? Only one combination of three words makes sense.
36 **words, spelling, school**
37 **writer, study, book**
38 **landed, broke, applause**
39 **sister, boyfriend, birthday**
40 **spent, weekend, lines**
41 **leave, depart** Both words mean to go or set off.
42 **bitter, sour** Both words mean tart or acidic.
43 **calm, peaceful** Both words mean relaxed or tranquil.
44 **sweep, brush** Both words mean to clean using a broom or brush.
45 **grateful, thankful** Both words mean full of gratitude.

Paper 19 (pages 53–56)

1 **same** Both the words mean very alike.
2 **say** Both the words mean to speak.
3 **let** Both the words mean to permit or consent to.
4 **beloved** Both the words mean adored or treasured.
5 **tree** A 'beech' is a type of 'tree'.

6 **OUR** courts
7 **RAN** warrant
8 **BAN** armbands
9 **HAD** shadow
10 **PEN** sharpen
11 **e** gate, ease
12 **t** mint, tact
13 **e** zone, etch
14 **t** bent, trim
15 **o** also, odds
16 **MV** The first letters move forwards three places and the second letters move backwards one place.
17 **8H** The numbers increase by 2 each time. The letters move forwards two places.
18 **ABD** All the letters move forwards two places.
19 **Nb** All the letters move forward one place. The first letter is always a capital (upper case) letter. The second letter is always lower case.
20 **7VU** The numbers decrease by 1 each time. Both the letters move backwards two places.

21

D	A	L	E
E		E	
A	L	A	S
L		P	

22

P	A	I	N
I		N	
N	O	T	E
T		O	

23

S	L	O	W
I			E
T	Y	P	E
E			K

24 **CASTLE**
25 **ANYONE**
26 **PIRATE**
27 **CINEMA**
28 **SHOPPING**

29–33 The only four-lettered word, NOTE, must be 6417. All the three-lettered words begin with 'T' except POT which must, therefore, be 541. From this, you can work out the remaining codes.

29 **145**
30 **541**
31 **144**
32 **146**
33 **6417**

34–37 Try each of the words in the first set of brackets. Do they make sense with any words in the second and third set of brackets? Only one combination of three words makes sense.

34 **queen, castle, crown**
35 **clock, on time, school**
36 **winter, snow, sledging**
37 **ill, medicine, better**
38 **nap**
39 **send**
40 **poke**
41 **soil**
42 **aunt**
43 **16** 1 + 2 + 6 + 7 = 16
44 **18** 8 + 7 + 2 + 1 = 18
45 **28** 6 + 8 + 7 + 7 = 28

Paper 20 (pages 57–59)

1 **D50** The letters move forward one place. The numbers increase by 5 each time.
2 **35D** The numbers increase by 2 each time. The letters move forward one place.
3 **DW** The first letters move forward one place. The second letters move backwards one place.
4 **GH** Both letters move forward two places.
5 **T** The letters move backwards one place.
6 **11** The number added increases by 1 each time: +1, +2, +3, +4
7 **32** The numbers decrease by 4 each time.
8 **20** The numbers increase by 5 each time.
9 **18** The numbers decrease by 3 each time.
10 **35** The numbers increase by 7 each time

11–15 Two of the three-letter words begin with the same letter so the missing code must be for RAN. ADD has a double 'D' so must be 266. Therefore AND = 256. As both the four-letter words begin with 'R', R = 4. Therefore RAN = 425. From this information, you can now work out the remaining letters.

11 **425**
12 **266**
13 **4275**
14 **4751**
15 **256**
16 **26** 5 + 6 + 7 + 8 = 26
17 **13** 5 + 3 + 4 + 1 = 13
18 **16** 7 + 2 + 4 + 3 = 16
19 **INCH, CHIN**
20 **BRUSH, SHRUB**
21 **NEAR, EARN**
22 **CLASP, SCALP**
23 **feet, teeth** I ran out of toothpaste so I couldn't brush my teeth.
24 **pig, dog** The dog barked to be let into the house.
25 **reason, fault** "It isn't my fault that the window is broken!"
26 **brief, short** Both words mean small or not long.
27 **glad, happy** Both words mean pleased or joyful.
28 **yell, scream** Both words mean to shriek or cry out.
29 **talk, speak** Both words mean to tell.
30 **see, look** Both words mean to observe or watch.
31 **BAT** battled
32 **HIP** spaceship
33 **OAR** soared
34 **LOW** followed
35 **RED** scored
36 **I** hail, lean
37 **t** most, time
38 **d** paid, drip
39 **t** belt, then
40 **e** cake, even
41 **helpless**
42 **setback**
43 **matchstick**
44 **message**
45 **indoors**

NOTES

21 four fork fire fall feel

If these words were placed in alphabetical order, which word would come fourth?

_____

22 If the letters in the following word are arranged in alphabetical order, which letter comes in the middle?

CHASE _____

2

Complete the following sentences by selecting the most sensible word from each group of words given in the brackets. Underline the words selected.

Example The (children, books, foxes) carried the (houses, books, steps) home from the (greengrocer, library, factory).

23 Mai took her (spoon, spade, hoe) to the (garden, beach, park) to build a (bridge, castle, palace).

24 The workman (knocked, fixed, tied) the (string, pipe, paper) to the (basin, cooker, table) in the bathroom.

25 No one (heard, wanted, bought) the (washing, burglar, road) enter the (kennel, fridge, house).

26 Can you (wait, hinder, help) me (empty, lift, buy) this box onto the (lawn, table, dog)?

27 The (monster, policeman, owl) (hooted, whispered, sang) in the (cupboard, hall, wood).

5

Which one letter can be added to the front of all these words to make new words?

Example care cat crate call

28 __hale __rap __in __art

29 __lame __right __one __urn

30 __lint __ray __rank __lea

31 __pen __at __pal __range

32 __lip __limb __heat __harm

5

Look at the first group of three words. The word in the middle has been made from the other two words. Complete the second group of three words in the same way, making a new word in the middle of the group.

Example PAIN INTO TOOK ALSO SOON ONLY

33	VEST	VEIN	PAIN	SOME	_____	TART
34	HARP	PART	PORT	GULP	_____	BARK
35	MASH	SHIP	TRIP	FIST	_____	GRAB
36	SELL	SEAT	BEAT	HOME	_____	RIPE
37	MARK	ARMS	HEMS	PEAL	_____	BUSY

5

Remove one letter from the word in capital letters to leave a new word. The meaning of the new word is given in the clue.

Example AUNT an insect ant

38	CLOUD	not quiet	_____
39	CLUB	a baby bear	_____
40	SHINE	part of the leg	_____
41	LIFE	a fib	_____
42	PANT	used for cooking	_____

5

43–45 In each list of words, the letters of one word have been jumbled up. Underline it and write it correctly.

FURNITURE	PARTS OF THE BODY	ANIMALS
piano	slip	mare
tools	nose	frog
table	eyes	toga
_____	_____	_____

3

Now go to the Progress Chart to record your score! **Total** 45

Paper 11

Fill in the crosswords so that all the given words are included. You have been given one letter as a clue in each crossword.

1

ever, done, opal, late

2

hats, need, tame, used

3

café, cart, fish, rush

3

Complete the following sentences by selecting the most sensible word from each group of words given in the brackets. Underline the words selected.

Example The (children, books, foxes) carried the (houses, books, steps) home from the (greengrocer, library, factory).

4 The old lady (smiled, yawned, laughed) because she was (tired, worried, ill) and wanted to go to (hospital, bed, play).

5 The (bike, ship, bed) (fell, swerved, ran) across the (pond, road, door).

6 He carefully (waited, cooked, climbed) through the (roof, garden, window) into the (zoo, kennel, castle).

7 She (climbed, shouted, turned) on the (lights, curtains, towels) as it was getting (light, dark, sunny).

8 Alex (hum, danced, clap) to the (rhythm, rhyme, tone) of the (music, chair, spoon).

5

Change one word so that the sentence makes sense. Underline the word you are taking out and write your new word on the line.

Example I waited in line to buy a book to see the film. ticket

9 I had a toothache so my mother took me to the hairdresser. _____

10 The swimming cage in my town has two diving boards. _____

11 When I asked my mum what a word meant she told me to look it up in the newspaper. _____

12 For lunch I like a cheese sandwich on brown rice and an apple. _____

13 My birthday candle this year is going to be chocolate sponge. _____ 5

If the code for PARENT is ACEGIK, what are the codes for the following words?

14 TREAT _____ 15 TEAR _____

16 PAN _____ 17 NEAT _____

What do these codes stand for?

18 KECA _____ 19 EGCA _____ 20 ACEK _____ 7

Change the first word of the third pair in the same way as the other pairs to give a new word.

Example bind, hind bare, hare but, hut

21 light, might line, mine list, _____

22 hair, air hand, and ball, _____

23 beach, reach best, rest bake, _____

24 oil, boil old, bold oat, _____ 4

Underline the pair of words most similar in meaning.

Example come, go roam, wander fear, fare

25 help, hinder hate, horrid burden, load

26 kind, thoughtful come, go top, hill

27 low, slight expect, hope come, depart

28 little, small fly, down top, bottom

29 last, ever one, once hide, conceal 5

Find the three-letter word which can be added to the letters in capitals to make a new word. The new word will complete the sentence sensibly.

Example The cat sprang onto the MO. USE

30 We keep the mower in the garden D. _____

31 The flowers are a bright OGE colour. _____

32 She peeled the apple and composted the S. _____

33 Some PS of the book were torn. _____

34 I like the yolk but not the WE of egg. _____ 5

Find the letter which will end the first word and start the second word.

Example peac (h) o m e

35 lon (__) ggs

36 bat (__) orn

37 mar (__) nit

38 pan (__) lse

39 mar (__) els 5

Find a word that can be put in front of each of the following words to make new, compound words.

Example cast fall ward pour down

40	side	crease	door	land	_____
41	cause	hind	neath	come	_____
42	side	shell	gull	bed	_____
43	side	standing	shine	right	_____
44	castle	pit	storm	paper	_____
45	port	bag	ship	craft	_____ 6

Now go to the Progress Chart to record your score! **Total** 45

Paper 12

1–5 Look at these groups of words.

Group A Tools
Group B Musical instruments
Group C Sports or games
Group D Vegetables

Choose the correct group for each of the words below. Write in the letter.

cricket __ peas __ axe __ drum __ saw __

guitar __ potatoes __ hammer __ piano __ football __

5

Find the letter which will end the first word and start the second word.

Example peac (h) ome

6 blo (__) ish **7** pas (__) pin **8** sho (__) ind

9 mus (__) idy **10** puf (__) eed

5

Underline two words, one from each group, that go together to form a new word. The word in the first group always comes first.

Example (hand, green, for) (light, house, sure)

11 (in, of, out) (fit, ill, well)

12 (was, be, do) (front, side, back)

13 (say, fare, end) (ill, gone, well)

14 (before, when, after) (come, wards, wet)

15 (check, pencil, pen) (down, side, out)

5

Complete the following expressions by underlining the missing word.

Example Frog is to tadpole as swan is to (duckling, baby, cygnet).

16 Aunt is to uncle as girl is to (boy, cousin, son).

17 Pupils are to teachers as patients are to (surgery, doctors, accident).

18 Dog is to puppy as cow is to (ram, lamb, calf).

19 Crowd is to people as flock is to (sheep, pigs, cows).

20 Pig is to sty as rabbit is to (drey, burrow, nest).

5

Fill in the crosswords so that all the given words are included. You have been given one letter as a clue in each crossword.

21

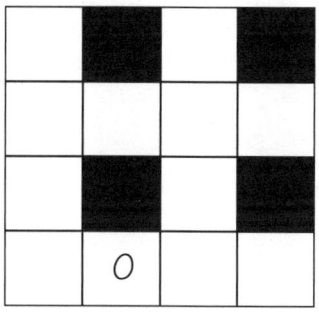

gone, news, snag, swan

22

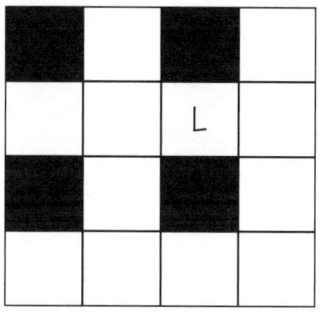

adds, apes, held, reap

23

cast, chew, even, shed

3

24 If the first five letters of the alphabet were removed, which would be the second letter of those left? Circle the correct letter.

E H G F

25 How many letters would there be in this alphabet? Circle the correct number.

20 21 22

26 Which month of the year begins with the sixth letter of the usual alphabet? _____

27 Which month of the year begins with the fourth letter? _____

4

If the code for STRAW is + − × ÷ @, what are the codes for the following words?

28 WAS _____ **29** RAW _____ **30** TAR _____

What do these codes stand for?

31 @ ÷ × _____ **32** + − ÷ × _____

5

33–35 Mr Young was 25 when Joshua was born. Complete the table.

Mr Young's age	27		35
Joshua's age		5	

3

Complete the following sentences by selecting the most sensible word from each group of words given in the brackets. Underline the words selected.

Example The (children, books, foxes) carried the (houses, books, steps) home from the (greengrocer, library, factory).

36 The (race, film, job) started when the (teacher, doctor, baker) blew her (crown, pencil, whistle).

37 My mum feeds the (birds, fish, cats) each morning by putting some (jam, seed, cake) out in the (car, bin, garden).

38 In our garden we have some (swings, rocks, flowers) in a (cup, pot, dish) that sits near the back (lake, road, door).

39 Jenny set the (chair, table, television) for supper by laying out the (books, pots, forks) and (pans, knives, apples).

40 The noise of the (bikes, trees, cars) as people go to (work, sleep, play) in the (morning, holiday, sun) wakes me.

5

Find and underline the two words which need to change places for each sentence to make sense.

Example She went to <u>letter</u> the <u>write</u>.

41 It is too outside to go cold today.

42 The fruit apple was made with grapes, pear and salad.

43 My aunt and uncle come and spend every holiday Christmas with us.

44 The police officer told the man to move his road because it was blocking the car.

45 Sometimes when I look out of my moon at night I can see the window.

5

Now go to the Progress Chart to record your score! **Total** 45

Paper 13

Fill in the crosswords so that all the given words are included. You have been given one letter as a clue in each crossword.

1

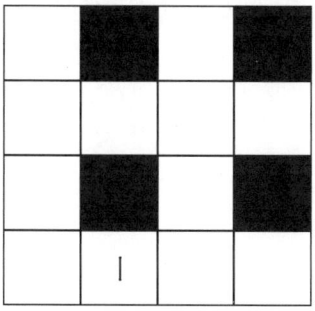

calm, peas, spit, time

2

also, hero, tail, tale

3

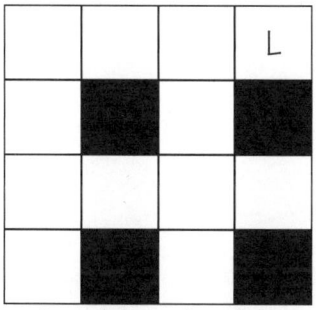

gate, girl, rude, tidy

3

Underline the pair of words most similar in meaning.

	Example	come, go	<u>roam, wander</u>	fear, fare
4	unhappy, sad	many, few	speak, listen
5	accept, refuse	divide, add	sharp, pointed
6	buy, sell	throw, catch	loud, noisy
7	cheap, inexpensive	generous, mean	rough, smooth
8	feeble, strong	give, take	terror, fear

5

Underline one word in the brackets which is most opposite in meaning to the word in capitals.

Example WIDE (broad vague long <u>narrow</u> motorway)

9 CHEERFUL (happy pleased sad joyful thoughtful)

10 EAT (meals starve hungry food dine)

11 MOVING (jump still run skip slow)

12 CLEAN (tint washed dirty dyed spill)

13 HELP (aid assist hinder flop earn)

5

If the letters in the following words are arranged in alphabetical order, which letter comes in the middle?

14 POUND _____

15 TRAIN _____

16 READS _____

17 AFTER _____

4

Remove one letter from the word in capital letters to leave a new word. The meaning of the new word is given in the clue.

Example AUNT an insect ant

18 DREAR at the back _____

19 SHORE painful _____

20 PLATE opposite of early _____

21 STALE a story _____

22 SINGE make a tune with the voice _____

23 PRIDE to go on horseback _____

6

If the code for SEASON is 135146, what are the codes for the following words?

24 NOSE _____ **25** SANE _____ **26** ONE _____

What do these codes stand for?

27 6446 _____ **28** 1446 _____

5

The pegs on one side of a cloakroom are numbered 1 to 20. On the other side they are numbered 21 to 40. 1 is opposite 21.

29 What number peg is opposite 8? __

30 What number peg is opposite 14? __

31 What number peg is opposite 39? __

3

Underline the one word which **cannot be made** from the letters of the word in capital letters.

Example	STATIONERY	stone	tyres	ration	nation	noisy
32	FLOWERS	slow	swore	fear	wore	flow
33	WANDER	wand	dear	draw	need	read
34	CURATE	rate	cater	rote	cart	care
35	MEANING	nine	main	game	none	mane
36	FASTEN	east	seat	neat	fate	star

5

Find a word that can be put in front of each of the following words to make new, compound words.

Example	cast	fall	ward	pour	down
37	pin	net	slide	dryer	_____
38	go	hand	mine	rate	_____
39	mate	yard	owner	shape	_____
40	roar	set	right	ward	_____
41	wheel	load	ridge	horse	_____

5

Houses 1 and 2 have green doors.

Houses 2 and 3 have brown windows.

Houses 1 and 4 have blue windows.

Houses 4 and 3 have red doors.

Which house has:

42 a green door and blue windows? _____

43 a red door and brown windows? _____

44 a green door and brown windows? _____

45 a red door and blue windows? _____

4

Now go to the Progress Chart to record your score! **Total** 45

Paper 14

Rearrange the muddled letters in capitals to make proper words. They are all colours.

1 KPIN _____ 2 YREG _____

3 YVAN _____ 4 AEUVM _____

5 NORWB _____ 5

Underline two words, one from each group, that go together to form a new word. The word in the first group always comes first.

Example (hand, green, for) (light, house, sure)

6 (old, hot, white) (paper, plate, petal)

7 (rain, snow, wet) (bow, arch, building)

8 (blood, tooth, pain) (hurt, sore, ache)

9 (big, leg, foot) (ball, park, shoe)

10 (fire, water, sea) (switch, alarm, place) 5

Add one letter to the word in capital letters to make a new word. The meaning of the new word is given in the clue.

Example PLAN simple plain

11 MIST to be damp _____

12 LOWER grows in the garden _____

13 FONT opposite of back _____

14 ROTS a horse does this _____

15 ROUND land _____ 5

Underline the two words, one from each group, which are the most opposite in meaning.

Exam (dawn, early, wake) (late, stop, sunrise)

16 (go, back, front) (here, for, come)

17 (moon, night, dark) (day, shadow, dawn)

18 (full, small, big) (over, tiny, empty)

19 (big, height, tall) (large, short, huge)

20 (play, lazy, good) (hard, cross, work)

5

Fill in the crosswords so that all the given words are included. You have been given one letter as a clue in each crossword.

21

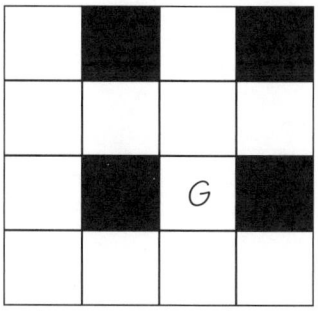

asks, sago, seat, spot

22

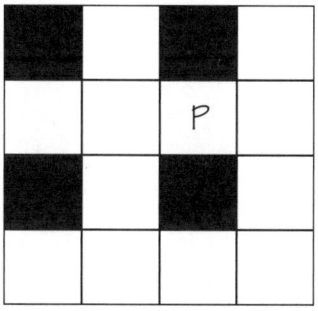

coop, hear, hope, spar

23

cart, chip, iron, root

3

Give the missing pairs of letters and numbers in the following sequences. The alphabet has been written out to help you.

A B C D E F G H I J K L M N O P Q R S T U V W X Y Z

	Example	CQ	DP	EQ	FP	GQ
24	AE	BF	__	DH	EI	
25	4D	5E	6F	7G	__	
26	ZB	YC	XD	__	VF	
27	2T	__	6R	8Q	10P	
28	__	KO	LN	MM	NL	

5

If the code for MASTER is + − × ÷ % @, what are the codes for the following words?

29 TEAM _____ **30** MET _____ **31** SET _____

What do these codes stand for?

32 + − × ÷ _____ **33** − @ + × _____ 5

If a = 2, b = 3, c = 4, d = 5, e = 6, f = 7, g = 8, h = 9, find the sum of these questions. Give your answers as letters.

34 (g + f) ÷ b = _____ **35** a + (h − b) = _____ **36** (c × e) ÷ g = _____ 3

Some children do a paper round.

Mike does Wednesday and Saturday. He sometimes does Monday as well.

Sally does Monday and Thursday. She never helps on Saturday.

Annie does Monday and Wednesday. She sometimes helps on Thursday.

Kim does Thursday and Saturday. She sometimes helps on Wednesday.

37 How many of the children work on Tuesday? _____

38 Who usually works on Wednesday but not Saturday? _____

39 Who works on Thursday but not Monday? _____

40 On which day of the week do Sally and Kim both work?

_____ 4

Underline the pair of words most similar in meaning.

Example come, go <u>roam, wander</u> fear, fare

41	unhappy, cross	tired, exhausted	run, skip
42	crawl, walk	sit, stand	swerve, dodge
43	mean, stingy	generous, poor	give, receive
44	army, navy	sea, harbour	soldiers, troops
45	first, last	first, tenth	double, twice

5

Now go to the Progress Chart to record your score! **Total** 45

Paper 15

Underline the two words which are the odd ones out in the following groups of words.

Example	black	<u>king</u>	purple	green	<u>house</u>
1 green	grass	blue	lawn	red	
2 wash	friend	pal	dry	mate	
3 cod	house	salmon	herring	cottage	
4 plate	cheese	dish	bread	butter	
5 shoe	glove	boot	hat	sandal	

5

Remove one letter from the word in capital letters to leave a new word. The meaning of the new word is given in the clue.

Example	AUNT	an insect	<u>ant</u>
6 FLIGHT	not heavy		_____
7 SWING	part of a bird		_____
8 CURVE	heal		_____
9 COAT	a pet		_____
10 HEAT	you wear it on your head		_____

5

Fill in the crosswords so that all the given words are included. You have been given one letter as a clue in each crossword.

11

heat, pony, rain, ship

12

army, fear, fete, very

13

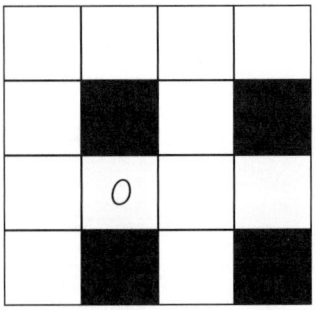

dote, late, wide, will

3

Change the first word of the third pair in the same way as the other pairs to give a new word.

Example bind, hind bare, hare but, hut

14 crane, cane plot, pot ship, _____

15 pat, peat wed, weed fat, _____

16 rats, star peek, keep stew, _____

17 lime, mile rite, tire care, _____

18 sit, sat clip, clap flit, _____

5

If a = 1, b = 2, c = 3, d = 4, find the value of the following.

19 a × b × c = __ **20** (b × d) − a = __ **21** c × d = __

3

Complete the following sentences by selecting the most sensible word from each group of words given in the brackets. Underline the words selected.

Example The (children, books, foxes) carried the (houses, books, steps) home from the (greengrocer, library, factory).

22 On my (day, morning, birthday) my (dog, cat, mother) makes me a special (biscuit, cake, bun).

23 The girl liked to (sleep, climb, eat) (cereal, milk, chips) with her (table, soup, fish).

24 The (night, pond, moon) was (wet, slow, heavy) and (sunny, dry, windy).

25 Don't (burn, bake, eat) the (stone, king, cake). It's been (baked, poisoned, lost)!

26 Few (sheep, goats, people) have ever (seen, grazed, stolen) the ruined (hedge, pond, city).

5

If the code for POTION is + − × ÷ − /, what are the codes for the following words?

27 POOP _____ **28** INTO _____ **29** OPTION _____

What do these codes stand for?

30 − / ÷ − / _____ **31** × ÷ / × _____ 5

Underline the word in brackets closest in meaning to the word in capitals.

Example UNHAPPY (unkind death laughter sad friendly)

32 CONTAIN (order help hold drop box)

33 LAST (first final try start ending)

34 WEALTHY (poor money banker rich cheque)

35 POST (wood stand box sign stake) 4

Underline the two words, one from each group, which are the most opposite in meaning.

Example (dawn, early, wake) (late, stop, sunrise)

36 (help, near, hope) (far, away, gone)

37 (save, money, box) (shop, keeper, spend)

38 (paint, brush, ugly) (colour, pretty, box)

39 (pat, like, friend) (unkind, sad, enemy)

40 (sound, quiet, song) (noisy, voice, sang) 5

Find and underline the two words which need to change places for each sentence to make sense.

Example She went to letter the write.

41 We went to the year for our holiday this sea.

42 Mike likes to go to his grandmother's school after house.

43 I forgot that had I checked a book out of the library.

44 It is important to look ways both when crossing the street.

45 I planted some seeds in the garden that I'd grown from flowers. 5

Now go to the Progress Chart to record your score! **Total** 45

Paper 16

Complete the following sentences by selecting the most sensible word from each group of words given in the brackets. Underline the words selected.

Example The (children, books, foxes) carried the (houses, books, steps) home from the (greengrocer, library, factory).

1 She was very (cross, tired, glad) and said (she, he, it) would like to (stand, sit, run) down.

2 My older (mother, aunt, sister) went to a (school, dance, bag) with her (suitcase, dog, boyfriend).

3 She (left, gave, ate) her (car, pancake, purse) in the (pond, sea, shop).

4 Can you (speak, tell, ring) for the (ambulance, trolley, driving) from your (free, mobile, call) phone?

5 After (breakfast, lunch, supper) the (keys, bikes, moon) came up in the (day, afternoon, sky). 5

Choose the word or phrase that makes each sentence true.

Example A LIBRARY always has (posters, a carpet, books, DVDs, stairs).

6 A FOREST always has (benches, a lake, paths, flowers, trees).

7 A PIG always has (a name, a tag, a sty, a tail, spots).

8 A HUSBAND is always a (father, man, worker, driver, golfer).

9 A NURSE always works (alone, in a hospital, with patients, at night, in a city).

10 A BOOK always has (illustrations, pages, a red cover, an index, a bookmark). 5

Underline any word which has the same letter three times.

11	December	Saturday	appears	potato
12	sparrow	trick	eleven	herring
13	individual	indeed	lesson	ironing
14	shines	eatable	release	gossip
15	necessary	alabaster	awkward	series

5

If the code for PLEASED is + − × ÷ = × /, what are the codes for the following words?

16 PLEAD _____ **17** APPLE _____ **18** PALE _____

What do these codes stand for?

19 / ÷ − × _____ **20** / × × / _____

5

Remove one letter from the word in capital letters to leave a new word. The meaning of the new word is given in the clue.

Example AUNT an insect ant

21 CREATE a box _____

22 SOLID bought by someone _____

23 WHOLE an opening _____

24 HEARD not soft _____

25 SUPPER great _____

5

Underline the word in the brackets closest in meaning to the word in capitals.

Example UNHAPPY (unkind death laughter sad friendly)

26 PUPILS (teacher parents friends children neighbours)

27 FELT TIPS (rulers writing books paper pens)

28 SOUNDS (whispers shouts silence noises cries)

29 HOUSE (office shed bungalow castle airport)

30 CHEST (arm leg box suitcase crate)

5

Underline the pair of words most opposite in meaning.

Example cup, mug coffee, milk hot, cold

31 beginning, end unkind, stern safe, alive

32 smooth, soft open, closed first, fast

33 pick, pack high, low short, call

34 strong, weak up, above eat, food

35 sleep, tired noise, shout quiet, loud

5

Find the three-letter word which can be added to the letters in capitals to make a new word. The new word will complete the sentence sensibly.

Example The cat sprang onto the MO. USE

36 My FRIS are all coming to my party. _____

37 Sixty MIES make an hour. _____

38 The building is very new and MRN. _____

39 We moved here three YS ago. _____

40 The police are offering a RED of £1000. _____ 5

In each line, underline the word that uses only the first 6 letters of the alphabet.

41	bake	bread	feed	abbot
42	black	face	dear	bale
43	band	aces	bead	abbey
44	fade	dream	dare	bake
45	deep	beak	bill	add

5

Now go to the Progress Chart to record your score! **Total** 45

Paper 17

Here is a weather chart showing hours of sunshine.

Average hours of sunshine per day

	Apr	May	Jun	July	Aug	Sept	Oct
Costa del Sol	8	10	11	11	11	9	7
Costa Brava	8	8	9	10	9	7	5
London	6	7	7	7	6	5	3

1 How many more hours of sunshine should the Costa Brava have each day in July compared with London? _____ hours.

2 How many hours of sunshine should London have altogether in the months mentioned? _____ hours.

3 What is the average (mean) hours of sunshine for the Costa Brava from April to October? _____ hours.

4 How many hours of sunshine should the Costa del Sol expect in May compared with the Costa Brava? ____ hours.

5 Over June, July and August, how many more hours of sunshine does the Costa del Sol have compared with London? _____ hours. 5

Underline the pair of words most opposite in meaning.

Example cup, mug coffee, milk hot, cold

6 sand, beach heavy, light tired, sleepy

7 run, around write, ink here, there

8 better, best whisper, shout read, write

9 late, early fish, meat cat, dog

10 talk, speak date, year glad, sad

5

Find the three-letter word which can be added to the letters in capitals to make a new word. The new word will complete the sentence sensibly.

Example The cat sprang onto the MO. USE

11 The runners RD each other to win. _____

12 The PAR is a bird usually kept in a cage. _____

13 'Do up the BUTS on your shirt!' _____

14 Tim liked BN sugar on his cereal. _____

15 Nishpa ENS the festival of Diwali. _____

5

Find the letter which will end the first word and start the second word.

Example peac (h) ome

16 han (__) eal

17 mat (__) nds

18 sal (__) wo

19 duc (__) now

20 mas (__) rack

5

Look at the first group of three words. The word in the middle has been made from the other two words. Complete the second group of three words in the same way, making a new word in the middle.

Example PAIN INTO TOOK ALSO SOON ONLY

21 HOME MEAN ANTS SANE _____ STAY

22 GREY EYES ESPY EACH _____ INCH

23 WEST WEAR ARTS BATH _____ SHED

24 LARK LINK SING BEST _____ NEAR

25 FIRE FISH SHOP BEAR _____ STEW

5

Underline the two words, one from each group, which are closest in meaning.

Example (race, shop, start) (finish, begin, end)

26 (fire, help, hinder) (call, after, aid)

27 (ruin, match, result) (mend, spoil, again)

28 (hate, angry, soft) (cross, hard, fallen)

29 (talk, chat, hear) (see, listen, cost)

30 (price, garment, till) (shop, label, cost)

5

Find the missing number by using the two numbers outside the brackets in the same way as the others sets of numbers.

Example 2 [8] 4 3 [18] 6 5 [25] 5

31 3 [9] 3 4 [8] 2 5 [__] 1

32 4 [5] 1 2 [7] 5 6 [__] 3

33 17 [3] 14 8 [3] 5 11 [__] 7

34 9 [12] 3 5 [12] 7 6 [__] 2

35 30 [6] 5 18 [6] 3 24 [__] 8

5

Underline the number that completes the sentence.

36 6 is to 36 as 7 is to (49, 28, 56)

37 12 is to 9 as 40 is to (12, 20, 30)

38 14 is to 21 as 21 is to (24, 28, 32)

39 4 is to 20 as 50 is to (80, 250, 100)

40 19 is to 38 as 38 is to (19, 76, 50)

5

Underline the word in brackets closest in meaning to the word in capitals.

Example UNHAPPY (unkind death laughter sad friendly)

41 PIP (fruit flower seed skin flesh)

42 FROSTY (cold snowy icy bright bitter)

43 SKID (roll trip slide tumble brake)

44 RAISE (upright tall lift drop collect)

45 LEAN (tilt bend fat hungry curve)

5

Now go to the Progress Chart to record your score! **Total** 45

Paper 18

1–5 Look at these groups of words.

Group A Kitchen things Group B Languages

Group C Birds Group D Animals

Choose the correct group for each of the words below. Write in the letter.

whisk __ camel __ Dutch __ scales __ gull __

German __ lamb __ recipe __ goose __ French __

5

Find the three-letter word which can be added to the letters in capitals to make a new word. The new word will complete the sentence sensibly.

Example The cat sprang onto the MO. USE

6 Have you seen the fish in the WR? _____

7 He was wearing a stripy SF. _____

8 You must SH the money with Nina. _____

9 Put the HING out to dry on the line. _____

10 No one saw him SL the money. _____

5

Find the letter which will end the first word and start the second word.

Example peac (h) ome

11 lan (__) own **12** fea (__) urn **13** gon (__) lass

14 sto (__) lace **15** rop (__) ar

5

Fill in the crosswords so that all the given words are included. You have been given one letter as a clue in each crossword.

16

eyes, yell, slop, sips

17

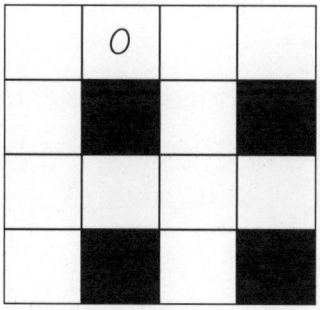

acts, flag, food, oats

2

Change the first word of the third pair in the same way as the other pairs to give a new word.

Example	bind, hind	bare, hare	but, hut
18 and, sand	ill, sill	eat, _____	
19 bet, best	cot, cost	lit, _____	
20 cat, coat	bat, boat	mat, _____	
21 fat, feat	mat, meat	hat, _____	
22 is, this	at, that	an, _____	

5

If the code for VEGETABLE is + / − / × @ $ = /, what are the codes for the following words?

23 GET _____ **24** BLEAT _____ **25** LEAVE _____

What do these codes stand for?

26 × @ − _____ **27** − @ × / _____

5

A and B wear blue jeans. C and B wear red shirts. D and A wear green shirts. C and D wear black jeans.

28 Who wore blue jeans and a red shirt? ___

29 Who wore black jeans and a green shirt? ___

30 Who wore blue jeans and a green shirt? ___

31 Who wore black jeans and a red shirt? ___

4

32 In each line, underline the word that uses only the first six letters of the alphabet.

dear cedar bead feast aside

1

If the following letters were arranged in alphabetical order, which letter comes in the middle?

33 CRIED _____

34 BROKE _____

35 SWEPT _____

3

Complete the following sentences by selecting the most sensible word from each group of words given in the brackets. Underline the words selected.

Example The (children, books, foxes) carried the (houses, books, steps) home from the (greengrocer, library, factory).

36 I studied my (words, letters, numbers) because we had a (running, art, spelling) test at (home, school, camp).

37 The (painter, butcher, writer) worked alone in her (car, study, desk) trying to finish her (poet, works, book).

38 When the plane (landed, swam, ran) we (waved, broke, dropped) into (silence, applause, cheers).

39 My (sister, brother, father) got a ring from her (cat, boyfriend, baby) for her (lunch, job, birthday).

40 The actress (found, lost, spent) the (second, weekend, years) learning her (lines, characters, costume). 5

Underline the pair of words most similar in meaning.

Example come, go roam, wander fear, fare

41	leave, depart	run, sit	sleep, awake
42	rough, smooth	half, whole	bitter, sour
43	messy, neat	calm, peaceful	rude, polite
44	sweep, brush	loose, tight	hungry, full
45	straight, crooked	grateful, thankful	less, more

5

Now go to the Progress Chart to record your score! Total 45

Paper 19

Underline the word in brackets closest in meaning to the word in capitals.

Example UNHAPPY (unkind death laughter sad friendly)

1 SIMILAR (different wrong same familiar smile)

2 TALK (shout say whisper argue cry)

3 ALLOW (stop low ask let all)

4 DEAR (sweet light honest dare beloved)

5 BEECH (sand sea tree plant branch)

5

Find the three-letter word which can be added to the letters in capitals to make a new word. The new word will complete the sentence sensibly.

Example The cat sprang onto the MO. USE

6 The tennis CTS were fully booked. _____

7 The police issued a WART for his arrest. _____

8 My sister wears ARMDS for swimming. _____

9 When the sun shines I can see my SOW. _____

10 I need to SHAR my pencil. _____

5

Find the letter which will end the first word and start the second word.

Example peac (h) ome

11 gat (__) ase

12 min (__) act

13 zon (__) tch

14 ben (__) rim

15 als (__) dds

5

Give the missing groups of letters and numbers in the following sequences. The alphabet has been written out to help you.

A B C D E F G H I J K L M N O P Q R S T U V W X Y Z

Example CQ DP EQ FP GQ

16 AZ DY GX JW ____

17 2B 4D 6F ____ 10J

18 ____ CDF EFH GHJ IJL

19 Ma ____ Oc Pd Qe

20 9ZY 8XW ____ 6TS 5RQ

5

Fill in the crosswords so that all the given words are included. You have been given one letter as a clue in each crossword.

21

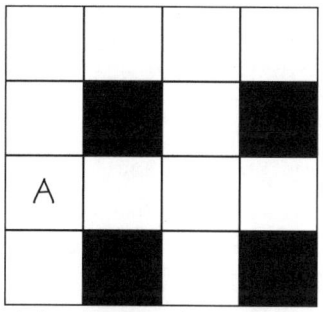

dale, leap, alas, deal

22

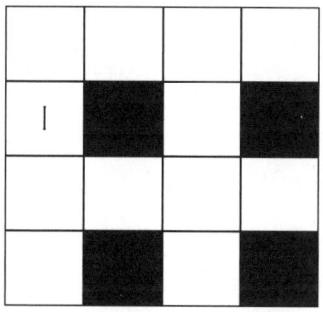

pain, into, note, pint

23

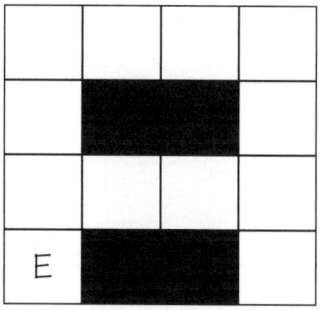

slow, site, week, type

3

Rearrange the muddled letters in capitals to make a proper word. The answer will complete the sentence sensibly.

Example A BEZAR is an animal with stripes. ZEBRA

24 We came at last to the ALECST gate. _____

25 Has AOEYNN seen my pen? _____

26 The IPREAT had a bag of money and a parrot. _____

27 We're going to the NICEAM tomorrow evening. _____

28 Please can you do the GNIPOPSH today? _____

5

These words have been written in code, but the codes are not under the right words.

TOP	POT	TOO	TON	NOTE
6417	144	146	541	145

Write the correct code for each word.

29 TOP _____ **30** POT _____ **31** TOO _____ **32** TON _____ **33** NOTE _____

5

Complete the following sentences by selecting the most sensible word from each group of words given in the brackets. Underline the words selected.

Example The (children, books, foxes) carried the (houses, books, steps) home from the (greengrocer, library, factory).

34 The (queen, king, prince) who lived in a (shed, train, castle) only wore her (hair, shoes, crown) for special occasions.

35 I set my alarm (pen, torch, clock) for seven o'clock because I wanted to be (on time, late, known) for my first day at (school, moon, tea).

36 During the (summer, winter, autumn) we sometimes get (snow, rain, clouds) which means we get to go (sledging, eating, sun bathing).

37 When I feel (well, ill, happy) my grandmother gives me some (medicine, trousers, glasses) to help me feel (sad, worse, better). 4

Remove one letter from the word in capital letters to leave a new word. The meaning of the new word is given in the clue.

Example AUNT an insect ant

38 SNAP a rest _____

39 SPEND to tell to go _____

40 SPOKE to push or jab _____

41 SPOIL dirt or earth _____

42 HAUNT a relative _____ 5

If the word DAUGHTERS is written in code as 123456789, what is the sum of these words?

43 D + A + T + E = _____

44 R + E + A + D = _____

45 T + R + E + E = _____ 3

Now go to the Progress Chart to record your score! **Total** 45

Paper 20

Complete these questions. The alphabet has been given to help you.

A B C D E F G H I J K L M N O P Q R S T U V W X Y Z

Example AB is to CD as PQ is to RS.

1 A35 is to B40 as C45 is to ____.

2 29A is to 31B as 33C is to ____.

3 AZ is to BY as CX is to ____.

4 AB is to CD as EF is to ____.

5 W is to V as U is to ____.

5

Fill in the missing number in each sequence.

Example 2 4 6 8 10

6 1 2 4 7 ___

7 40 36 ___ 28 24

8 5 10 15 ___ 25

9 24 21 ___ 15 12

10 7 14 21 28 ___

5

These words have been written in code, but the codes are not under the correct words. One code is missing.

RAN	ADD	RAIN	RING	AND
4751	4275	256	266	

Write the correct code for each word.

11 RAN ____ 12 ADD ____ 13 RAIN ____ 14 RING ____ 15 AND ____

5

If the word MARIGOLD is written in code as 12345678, what is the sum of these words?

16 G + O + L + D = ____ 17 G + R + I + M = ____

18 L + A + I + R = ____

3

Underline the two words which are made from the same letters.

Example TAP PET TEA POT EAT

19 INCH CHAP CHIN NICE PACK

20 CRUSH SHUSH BRUSH SHRUB BUNCH

21 RAIN NEAT NEAR EARN TENT

22 CLASP CLASS SCORE PLACE SCALP

4

Change one word so that the sentence makes sense. Underline the word you are taking out and write your new word on the line.

Example I waited in line to buy a book to see the film. ticket

23 I ran out of toothpaste so couldn't brush my feet. _____

24 The pig barked to be let into the house. _____

25 'It isn't my reason that the window is broken!' _____

3

Underline the pair of words most similar in meaning.

Example come, go roam, wander fear, fare

26 young, old brief, short good, bad

27 in, out better, worse glad, happy

28 dark, light yell, scream colour, plain

29 talk, speak cold, hot bed, time

30 read, story see, look eat, food

5

Find the three-letter word which can be added to the letters in capitals to make a new word. The new word will complete the sentence sensibly.

Example The cat sprang onto the MO. USE

31 We TLED through the crowds. _____

32 The SPACES landed on the moon. _____

33 The eagle SED effortlessly. _____

34 We FOLED the path to the sea. _____

35 The player SCO a goal. _____

5

Find the letter which will end the first word and start the second word.

Example peac (h) ome

36 hai (__) ean

37 mos (__) ime

38 pai (__) rip

39 bel (__) hen

40 cak (__) ven

5

Underline two words, one from each group, that go together to form a new word. The word in the first group always comes first.

Example (hand, green, for) (light, house, sure)

41 (birth, help, cradle) (less, more, much)

42 (pick, slow, set) (end, back, forward)

43 (in, smoke, match) (fire, water, stick)

44 (dirty, mess, clean) (time, old, age)

45 (let, come, in) (room, doors, stairs)

5

Now go to the Progress Chart to record your score! **Total** 45

Progress Chart Verbal Reasoning 8–9 years

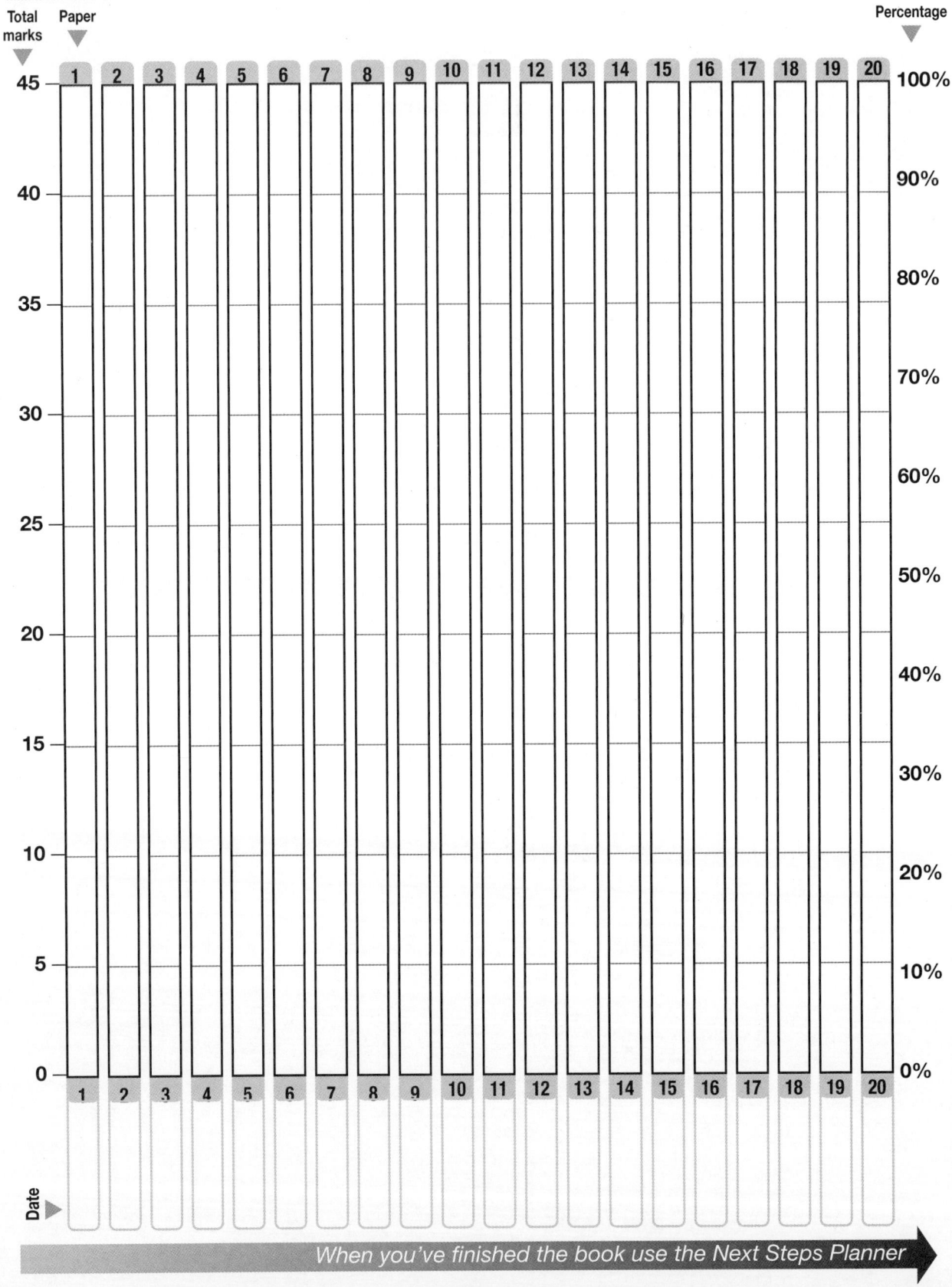

When you've finished the book use the Next Steps Planner